"A cogent and comprehensive discussion of the retirement challenge clearly written by an experienced advisor. A must read for pre-retirement planning."

—*Michael Tate, CFP®,*
Bay Area Wealth Management Group, Wealth Manager

"This book helps you plan a successful and fulfilling retirement. It's well-written with many examples and delightful vignettes. A well-researched read that will gives ideas, opportunities and details to plan a splendid retirement. Adding to the book's impact are the Appendices that provide a great deal of practical information. "

—*Jan M. Schmuckler, PhD, Author of Role Montage:*
A Creative New Way to Discover the LEADER Within You,
Retired Director of the JFKU Graduate Coaching Program
and Former Professor of Organizational Behavior

RETIREMENT SAVVY

SAVVY

Designing Your Next Great Adventure

Denise P. Kalm

ABOOKS
Alive Book Publishing

Retirement Savvy
Copyright © 2019 by Denise P. Kalm

Additional copies may be ordered from the publisher for educational, business, promotional or premium use.
For information, contact ALIVE Book Publishing at:
alivebookpublishing.com, or call (925) 837-7303.

Book Design by Alex Johnson

ISBN 13
978-1-63132-079-1

Library of Congress Control Number: 2019918699

Library of Congress Cataloging-in-Publication Data
is available upon request.

First Edition

Published in the United States of America by ALIVE Book Publishing
and ALIVE Publishing Group, imprints of Advanced Publishing LLC
3200 A Danville Blvd., Suite 204, Alamo, California 94507
alivebookpublishing.com

PRINTED IN THE UNITED STATES OF AMERICA

10 9 8 7 6 5 4 3 2 1

To my mother, Louise Hitchcock,
who taught me to live each day
as if it were my last
and to cherish every moment.
She enjoyed her last adventure 20 years ago.
I still miss her.

Contents

Foreword...9

Introduction...13

DREAMING BIG

Chapter 1 - What does it Mean to Retire?.....................19

Chapter 2 - Who Are You Now?..................................23

Chapter 3 - What Are Your Needs?.............................27

Chapter 4 - Finding Your Happiness Intersection...........33

Chapter 5 - Aligning with Your Values.........................39

Chapter 6 - Mining Your Bucket List............................45

Chapter 7 - Traveling Well..49

Chapter 8 - To Work ... or Not?.................................57

Chapter 9 - Volunteering..63

FOCUSING ON THE DETAILS

Chapter 10 - Importance of Plans, Schedules and Lists...71

Chapter 11 - Maintaining Your Health..........................77

Chapter 12 - Maintaining Your Brain............................87

Chapter 13 - Reclaiming Your Creativity.......................93

Chapter 14 - Discover and Add New Strengths..............97

Chapter 15 - To Move or Not......................................101

Chapter 16 - Ways to Stay Connected.......................109

Chapter 17 - Syncing with Your Partner......................115

COURSE CORRECTIONS

Chapter 18 - Becoming a Caregiver...........................123

Chapter 19 - Divorce..129

Chapter 20 - Adapting to Your Own Aging..................133

Conclusion..139

Acknowledgements..141

APPENDICES

Appendix A - Medicare Basics..................................145

Appendix B - Phone and Internet Safety....................153

Appendix C - My Supplements.................................157

Appendix D - Useful Links.......................................159

About the Author...161

Foreword

My interest in retirement began with a course I took in law school in 1980 titled Pensions. For my final paper, I compared and contrasted various types plans. The difference in results from one plan to another made an impression on me. I saw the benefit of starting early with contributions, monitoring the investments along the way, and projecting the anticipated retirement distributions. But one thing we didn't learn: will it be sufficient for the retiree's cash flow needs? And what will those needs be?

Three years later, I joined my father in the brokerage/investment advisory business and was able to show retirement cash flow models to our clients. But in order to do this, the first major issue is to understand the client's lifestyle goals, travel dreams, health cost needs, and much more. I went on to earn other retirement focused credentials, all adding more insight and guidance in helping clients to design their life in retirement and not live it by default. I continued my education adding money and retirement coaching to the mix.

Over the years, I was asked by many colleagues to review their manuscripts for publication, provide book reviews for published works, and offered authoring and editing opportunities as a contributor to other works, all in the area of retirement planning. I've got quite an accumulation on my bookshelf, and now I'm looking forward to adding one more – this book by my friend, Denise!

Denise and I met around 2006 through the East Bay Coaches, a local chapter of the International Coaching Federation (ICF). I was beginning the next chapter of my life as a Certified Money Coach (CMC)^{SM}, helping people with their subconscious money beliefs and resulting challenging patterns of behavior. I felt that a good way to gain more and better coaching skills was to be in the company of other types of professional coaches through ICF.

My friendship with Denise (and her husband) grew through this association, and, living in the same area, we bumped into each other now and then, keeping each other up to date on things happening in our lives. I've always been impressed by her life story – how she got into writing, what drew her to technical authorship, her shift into coaching, her creativity and passion, and her zest for life.

When I got an email from her asking me to review her book, I jumped at the opportunity! After reading the manuscript, I didn't think a quote would best express my feelings about it and I asked if I might be blessed with the opportunity to write this foreword.

Denise's book is a very easy read, and I found it hard to put down. It so well covers the concepts I had employed years ago and was now providing as a Certified Professional Retirement Coach (CPRC) ^{SM}. Another friend from years back created a new and accredited certification program for retirement coaching, and what Denise covers in her book includes much of what that program coursework teaches coaches-in-training to consider when working with their clients. I see great value in my clients reading this book in conjunction with my coaching work with them to design their next great adventure.

Retirement planning is much more than money – it's a look inside yourself to see and accept the truth of who you really are and what's next for you in this magical part of life where having to go to work every day is not part of the agenda. This book will help you plan your journey.

Steven "Shags" Shagrin, JD
Certified Money Coach (CMC)^{SM}
Certified Professional Retirement Coach (CPRC)^{SM}
Certified Retirement Planning Counselor (CRPC)^{SM}
Registered Life Planner (RLP) ®
Past President, International Society for
Retirement & Life Planning
Editor, Facts About Retiring in the United States
(The H.W. Wilson Company, 2001)

Introduction

The concept of freedom is never truly realized until one settles into retirement mode.
—A. Major, writer

I'm one of you, a woman of 'a certain age,' storm-tossed on the ocean of job layoffs, thinking about retirement after years of trying to make entrepreneurship work for me. I'd reinvented myself many times, beginning my work life as a scientist, working my way through a variety of roles in information technology (IT), getting my coaching certificate at night in my '50s. I thought figuring out retirement would be easy: just one more reinvention. But as I began to consider my options, I used my coaching process on myself. First, I did a lot of research and talked to people who had already retired, successfully or not. I did some retirement coaching. I'm planning my next great adventure with you and truly believe that my best years are still ahead. Come with me—it's going to be a great ride!

Maria dreamed about getting enough sleep and time to herself after she retired. Her job as chief of staff to the CEO of a software company in downtown Boston meant being on-call 7x24, running errands, attending industry events and working unconscionable hours. Having given up her life to make her boss look good, she relished the prospect of having no demands and no one to please. After a few months, she discovered that many of her friends weren't available to spend time with her. Visions of ladies' lunches, card parties and other casual fun dimmed when she realized how lucky she had been to retire so early. Most confessed to needing to stash away more money before quitting.

At 70, her best friend, Renee, looked wrung out, broken by the physical demands of her beloved nursing job. But she had no choice; her husband's health had stolen their savings before illness took him from her. Feeling guilty about being bored, Maria didn't share her despair with anyone, but she wondered where her joy had gone. The days stretched on, shapeless, drifting by like a wisp of cloud.

Land-bound in Nebraska by his career, Jerry spent every vacation sailing in one exotic location after another. Carefully saving his money, he bought a small property in the Cayman Islands and a sailboat he could sail by himself. He retired at 62, hoping to get a few great years in before his family medical history caught up with him. The first two weeks were heaven: eat breakfast on his deck, go out for a morning sail, make lunch, fish, eat fish, sleep.

The third week, he began to feel sailing had become a job. He found himself getting up later, rebelling against the 'demand' the boat presented. What had been pleasure had become obligation. He did love sailing, but he realized that sailing could never be his reason for living; it wasn't enough.

"I planned it out for so long," he told his brother. But he really hadn't planned at all. As a visitor to the islands, he never realized how little interest the Caymanians had in mingling with outsiders. Making friends proved almost impossible. Jerry was lonely and bored.

Does retirement simply mean not working? Does it mean lying around doing very little? As I got older and saw so many options to consider, I found myself deferring any decisions. But then my friends began to retire and they shared their stories with me. As someone who had figured out how to plan a successful career, I needed to figure out the rules for a great retirement, for my friends, my readers and myself. As I researched this book, a few key observations drove my plan.

Baby Boomers and those who follow are entering into a new concept of retirement; we have to reinvent it for ourselves. Where once ailing seniors sought out a soft porch chair to rest their aging bodies, worn down from years of physical toil, most of us now retire younger and healthier. In many cases, our jobs are less physically taxing, we are in better shape health-wise and we have a much longer lifespan. But will we enjoy it?

Recognize that the US Government set the Social Security age at 65 back when many people didn't live to 65, and most of those who did had very few years left to enjoy their retirement. Now, we probably have 30+ years ahead of us when we hit that "magic age," almost as many years as the number we worked. What should we do with all that time? And more importantly, what can we make of that time for ourselves to bring us fulfillment and joy?

Each person has their own view of retirement. One dictionary defines retirement as "the action or fact of leaving one's job and ceasing to work." Many people just expect that this is all it is, the absence of work. But is that enough for you? Can't we do better? Why not redefine the period we look forward to enjoying and make a plan for a life we will love?

Call it your 'second act,' or just your next great adventure. Retirement is not for raising a family, building a career and saving money. It is a new beginning, a chance to focus on yourself and your own desires. But, while many people have done well in creating a great retirement account, not as many have made a plan for what they'll do in retirement. We have to take advantage of the early years while we still have our health, yet we have to be mindful of wealth preservation for the long years ahead, where health care may eat up more of our savings.

We planned our careers, yet too often only have a list of "*don'ts*" and "*won'ts*" as a retirement plan. "I won't have to commute anymore. I don't need to dress up every day. I won't worry about playing politics." While true, "won'ts" aren't a plan of action to make the most of those valuable years. What will you do next?

Start with your dreams to plan a retirement that will satisfy you. However, as you can see from Jerry's story, having a great retirement is more than just going for one dream. Realtors caution you not to make your last move without really checking out the place. The same guidelines are true for every aspect of a quality retirement. As most of us do not grow up to be the ballerinas and firemen of our childhood wishes, those who find fulfillment in the latter years of their lives also take the time to assess, test and plan for those years.

Retirement Savvy will help you plot a course for a satisfying, fulfilling and wonderful retirement, whether you never earn another nickel or prefer to explore a career goal everyone told you not to try. This book isn't a financial planning guide; there are many of those out there. Instead, we'll look at all the pieces to the puzzle of making it a retirement you will enjoy and relish by helping you to connect with your passions, values and needs. In the process, you will read stories of what does and doesn't work, which highlight each planning stage. Make some notes as you read along. These notes will help you make your own plan. A great life doesn't simply happen; it only happens when you create a plan and then execute it. The result will be the life you have earned and know you deserve – a fulfilling and enlightening retirement.

> *God gave us the gift of life; it is up to us to give*
> *ourselves the gift of living well.*
> —Voltaire, writer

DREAMING BIG

Chapter 1

What does it Mean to Retire?

Retirement means doing what you have fun doing.
– Dick Van Dyke, actor

Only a few years back, everyone seemed to have a clear idea of what it meant to retire. You picked a date, let your company know, and began transitioning work to other team members. Often, the company would celebrate your career end with a party and/or a gift. You could officially say, "I'm retired."

With so many changes in the work world, while some may find that they can follow that pattern, many cannot.

Shannon had successfully managed her career, making strategic job changes and elevating her influence and compensation accordingly throughout the years. Despite two midlife layoffs, Shannon quickly found new jobs and kept her career on track. Always on top of things, she had decided to retire when she turned 66 and four months, when she would reach her full retirement age under the new rules of Social Security. She longed to move out of Chicago to a mountain cabin somewhere peaceful.

Celebrating her 63rd birthday in October, she got an early birthday 'present'; her company gave her notice on September 30th.

"We're rethinking our direction," said the HR director. He declined to give her any further information on the reasoning. Security guards escorted her out, a walk of shame she hoped she would never have to repeat.

Weeks passed. Shannon didn't score even a single screening interview. She consulted an attorney, hoping to find that she could sue her former employer for age discrimination or go after the companies who wouldn't even speak to her.

"Every one of them asks an age-related question on the application. Most just want the year you graduated from high school, but others ask your birthdate. Isn't that illegal?"

The attorney frowned his frustration clear. "Yes, but ... Companies will almost always lay off someone much younger to 'balance out' the numbers and prove they aren't discriminating. And part of their reasoning is that older workers are paid more.

"You can try to sue the companies you apply to, but in reality we have almost no success in these actions. It's very costly for you and likely to result in years of litigation. And you'll probably lose your severance if you do."

Shannon didn't know her next move. Was she retired? She had her severance and could apply for unemployment, but none of that would get her through to her planned date. Nor would COBRA last long enough to get her to Medicare.

The unchosen retirement is increasingly common and can leave a person feeling stuck. It's like having geared up to run a 10K and being pulled out of the race after the first mile. What do I do now?

Being self-employed presents challenges as well. After years of working, I found myself in Shannon's shoes, though I was younger. The market was particularly tough in 2012. I didn't want to deal with the 2 ½ hour each-way commute to Silicon Valley, and yet I didn't feel I could retire. Instead, I started my own business and soon discovered the ebb and flow of work when you must constantly find new consulting gigs.

Soon after I started this, some friends referred to me as

retired, which I deeply resented, given the hours I put in. Some months, the work slowed down a lot, making me wonder if I should actually retire. Used to the constant stress of work overload at the software companies I had worked for, the cyclical nature of my work felt scary while also freeing. In between, I could do whatever I wanted to. If only I knew for sure what that looked like.

Turning 65 as I wrote this, I began to consider retiring. But my vision of what I would do when I no longer had my corporation included continuing to do outplacement coaching for a firm, writing the occasional blog for my remaining client, continuing to write books and finding a way to do career coaching for veterans—my passion project. But wait. Isn't that working? I started tasting the word "retirement" as if I could figure it out if I said it enough. I realized that when we have the energy, intelligence, stamina and drive to do more, retirement couldn't be the right word anymore. A second life? A new beginning? I felt I was on verge of inventing something.

What does retirement mean for you? This has to be the first question you ask as you consider whether to retire (or whether, like Shannon or me, you find that work has abandoned you.) Succeeding chapters represent my journey as well as yours, as we work to figure out what we want to be when we get to make all the choices and begin to have more fun.

Retirement, a time to do what you want to do,
when you want to do it, where you want to do it, and,
how you want to do it.
— Catherine Pulsifer, writer

Chapter 2

Who Are You Now?

The trouble with retirement is that you never get a day off.
—Abe Lemons, basketball player and coach

Many of us have spent our lives defined by our jobs. The first thing we do after introducing ourselves is to tell a new friend what we do for a living. As people discover when they get laid off, suddenly having no role can be jarring. For some, it poses an identity crisis. For others, it just becomes an awkward moment when people ask about their work. But for retirees, it can be equally confusing. Who am I now? Who do I want to be? As noted in the introduction, ceasing to work is not an activity; it marks the end of your current job. That's not enough for many of us.

Rohani felt she had too many roles in her life: mother, wife, bookkeeper, and volunteer for Meals on Wheels. Her kids finally landed on their feet and left the family home; she gave up her volunteer work because she no longer enjoyed the huge driving demands required in her rural community in southern Tennessee. She was burned out on everything and really looked forward to doing nothing for a while.

For a few weeks, she enjoyed filling her backpack with library books and then sitting in her garden for hours just reading. She woke late, made more casual meals, and did laundry only when she and her husband were running out of options. Even when she tried to plan something, she found it hard to find the time to get it done. It seemed as if time had sped up

—Rohani felt like she had done nothing since her farewell party.

Her best friend, Merced, called her one weekend, hoping to catch up over coffee. "What are you doing with yourself?" she asked. Merced had to work: she had aging parents who hadn't saved enough and adult children who still needed her help. Rohani flushed; she wanted a purpose. Merced had a reason to get up each day; she didn't.

Rohani needed a plan. In another case, Mark needed a new definition of retirement for himself.

Mark didn't really "retire." Friends kept talking about him as retired, but he resented it. He still worked, just not as much as he had before. He had a small business in a suburb of Pittsburgh, PA as a locksmith and, over time, cut his hours and stopped doing emergency work. Instead, he finally got to coach softball, a passion he had wanted to indulge in when his kids were young, but never had the time. He felt conflicted. Is this retirement? Am I still working? He felt he had made the right decision, giving himself more choice in his life, but was he a retiree or just a part-time worker? His best friend, Leo, was driving for Uber, mostly because he enjoyed the conversations and sharing his expertise on how to enjoy the sights in Pittsburgh. Was Leo retired?

Who do you want to be now that you're retired? Our experiences and roles have assigned us a variety of "brands," labels which define our purpose at various life stages. We might have several identities at various times in our lives: mother, teacher, nurse, attorney. Or contractor, soccer coach, photographer, TV junkie. In our post- career world, we get to define our purpose and our brand to be whatever we want. Even better, you're never locked in. Change your identity and/or have several brands depending on what role you are playing now. But remember: you only control who you are when you make a choice. Don't let anyone else define you.

Rohani had lost her work-life identity and, when considering her purpose, realized that she wanted to be more than the weekly library visitor she had become. She had forgotten to make a plan. Mark didn't like to be called "retired," which he took to mean that he had given up. But who was he now?

When you have a clear vision of who you want to be, you have clarity about the near future. We can find ourselves "branded" by others' expectations when we don't make a choice. Retired is not a useful term because it has no real meaning. To be able to successfully execute your plan, having a clear idea of what you want is not enough. You need to communicate it to your family and friends so they know who you are now and understand how to respect your time.

Our 40+ hours of work per week gave our days a structure that allowed us to slot in everything we needed and wanted to get done around those hours. When you wake with no plan, it's easy to have the day slip away. Knowing who you want to be at this point in time helps you create a plan. Otherwise, it's easy to not even get the basics done, such as house cleaning or minor repairs.

The next few chapters provide tools which are essential in crafting and refining your retirement vision, showing how you have the opportunity to make a lot of new choices. If you have sufficient money, perhaps you'll stop suffering the pains of the 'honey-do' list or give up many of the things you had to do yourself as a parent. What does it feel like to chart a path based on what you want right now, instead of what you have to do? How empowering is that? We need a new set of terms to describe ourselves. We're not either working or retired. We can be whatever we choose to be.

The goal isn't to create a strict plan you must live by, but to open your mind to the possibilities. Probably the most empowering part is that, whatever choice you make, you can change it at the drop of a hat. Unlike a career, no one is going to look at your resume anymore and challenge the path you've carved out. Given that some of us will have nearly as many years in retirement as we did in the work world, it only makes sense to plan our second act with thought as often as needed.

Retirement is the beginning of life, not the end.
—Ernie Zelinski, writer

Chapter 3

What Are Your Needs?

What will I do with myself when I retire? When I quit my job, I do not want to quit living. Can I possibly be of use when retirement day comes, or will I just be taking up space?
—J. A. West, writer

Before creating a plan, it is helpful to understand something about your needs. While some of these topics will be discussed in later chapters, it helps to have a common base with which to work. Maslow's Hierarchy of Needs is a great model as it tracks well with the choices you will want to make in the next few years. Though originally designed to assess childhood development, the model offers a way to understand what needs must be satisfied to ensure you move up the pyramid from stress needs to pleasure needs. The design implies that you need to satisfy each level to get to the next. Achieving a great retirement means moving to the top of the pyramid.

The most basic needs are "physiological." If these aren't met, life will be shorter and more challenging, which is not anyone's idea of a good life. While most of us may have these factors under control, you can't lose sight of them. As we begin to plan our chosen activities, we want to make sure that we can always keep a roof over our heads and food in the fridge.

The second level of needs is "safety." There are many books about investing for retirement and financial options you have; money will not be a subject of this book. But if you haven't planned carefully enough, you may have to adjust your dreams or consider part-time work to fill the gap. But safety isn't just about money.

Figure 1. Maslow's Hierarchy of Needs[1]

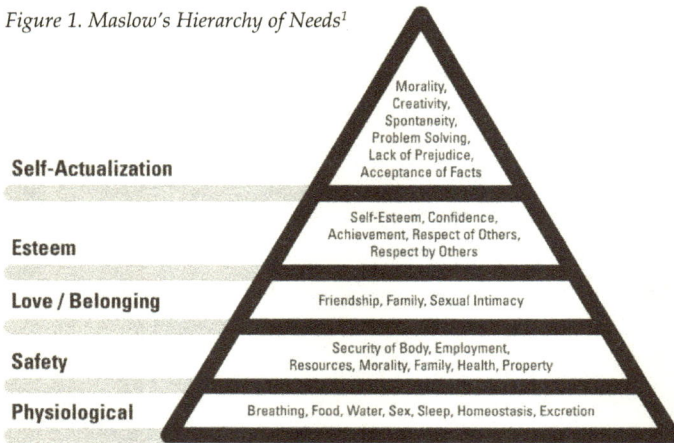

Self-Actualization — Morality, Creativity, Spontaneity, Problem Solving, Lack of Prejudice, Acceptance of Facts

Esteem — Self-Esteem, Confidence, Achievement, Respect of Others, Respect by Others

Love / Belonging — Friendship, Family, Sexual Intimacy

Safety — Security of Body, Employment, Resources, Morality, Family, Health, Property

Physiological — Breathing, Food, Water, Sex, Sleep, Homeostasis, Excretion

For many, safety means looking for a safer, more affordable place to live such as a gated community in a low-crime city. Maybe it's time to get rid of your car and opt for delivery services instead. Over the long haul, delivery will be safer and may even be a lot cheaper. We might want to opt for a security system, a video doorbell and more. At the same time, consider the risks of WiFi internet connectivity. It may be time to upgrade to more security with your devices. Internet safety is covered in Appendix B.

We also want to be close to the resources we need, such as hospitals, airports, a health club, grocery stores, etc. A resource is defined as whatever you need to feel safe and cared for.

Health may be the biggest safety need as we age. Almost everyone encounters those unwelcome medical "surprises." Joints that once operated smoothly start aching. Names and nouns elude us when we try to access them. Eyesight dims

---

[1] A.H. Maslow. "A Theory of Human Motivation," *Psychological Review*, 50(4), 370–96, 1943.

and hearing diminishes. Fine-finger movements, like the ones I need for cross-stitch, become a struggle. The body we relied on without a thought no longer works as it did. Health also impacts our choices.

Slower reflexes mean you probably want to alter your driving style to adjust. I try to be more patient, giving myself more time to react. I plan more, ensuring enough there's time to get to where I'm going.

Leslie and Brad had always loved the Mendocino coast. In retirement, they couldn't quite swing the beachfront property they dreamed about, but found a home just off the Anderson Valley wine trail which gave them easy access to the coast. It felt like a dream come true. Peaceful drives up to Ft. Bragg, picnics at favorite wineries – what could be better? One day, walking on a beach near Little River, Brad grabbed his chest and fell to the ground, clearly in pain. They'd both had a good checkup the year before, but it looked to Leslie as if Brad had just experienced his first heart attack.

She dialed 911 on her cell phone, feeling lucky to get a signal in that remote site. The wait for help seemed endless. When the paramedics finally arrived, they did what they could, but Brad needed an emergency bypass. The closest hospital was miles away in Santa Rosa; a helicopter ride had to be arranged. While waiting for the chopper to arrive, she watched the EMTs try to keep her husband alive. Leslie panicked. Why had they given up their nice condo near a hospital? What would she do without him? Suddenly, nothing mattered but keeping him alive and with her.

Arriving by helicopter, the doctor called the time of death within minutes. It simply took too long to get help.

A month later, Leslie got a bill for the helicopter and gasped at the amount. A neighbor sighed and said, "Yeah, we all pay for insurance to get a ride. It makes it affordable, but even so, a helicopter may not be fast enough."

Retirement has to include a way to feel safe, which may change where you choose to live.

Once you have the two basic needs fulfilled, the higher-level needs may not seem obvious but deserve our attention. "Love and belonging" are core needs for retirees, as for everyone else, but can be harder to achieve. Work provided many of us with our friends and even, in some cases, our future mates. Now, we have to "work" at making friends again. Every year, it can be more challenging. I remember how easy it was to meet people when I went to school. While you might speak to a variety of people throughout the day, making deeper connections takes more work.

Whether you choose to move or not, friends and family may move and leave you behind. Close buddies drift apart as dreams diverge or health issues intervene. Death becomes a more frequent visitor, stealing away the ones you love. And yet, most of us want a variety of people in our lives. As we assess our plans, we need to consider how we can keep connected and a part of the human network.

"Esteem" needs shouldn't be ignored. For a lot of us, work offered benefits beyond the paycheck. Most people enjoy feeling valued and rewarded for their expertise and hard work. Although we might hesitate to admit it, most of us really want to feel needed. As we age, many around us may feel we need to be helped, but ask someone who has been retired a while. When someone needs their help, or simply an ear, the experience is rejuvenating and rewarding. Remember this when you help your aging parents. They need to feel useful too.

Achievement goals will change, but we all need to feel we have accomplished something. I remember how great it felt to complete a project at work or finish the draft of a book. Your need for this won't vanish when you finally leave the office, so you'll want to redefine the words "achievement" and "accomplishment." It may be simply getting that storage locker empty or finally creating your living trust. Just as you enjoyed the feeling when you worked, you'll relish the feeling of a job well done.

Finally, Maslow describes a need called "self-actualization," a need he believed most would never achieve. His standards were very high and a bit unrealistic. In coaching practice, I believe that this level is not only readily achievable but highly desirable. In the fabric of life, self-actualization is how smoothly you have woven your choices together and how the fabric looks when viewed as a whole instead of as individual choices.

Imagine that you have set out on a journey, perhaps in that plush new RV you've bought. You have the idea that you will just drive the roads and see what you might see. For a while, the journey is pleasant, but with no plan and no direction, it can begin to feel aimless. The petty annoyances of road travel begin to outweigh the adventure. You don't know when your journey ends or how it ends, and you may begin to care very much about these things.

Some novelists write books without a plan or direction, figuring they'll just know how it ends. When we read these books, we can feel let down because the end simply falls off a cliff. Rather than leaving us with a deeper understanding, a new perspective or simply the feeling that a story has been fulfilled, we feel cheated. Your retirement, if unplanned, can be that uncharted journey, that badly conceived novel where the end, when it comes, is disquieting and disappointing. You can do better.

Don't act your age [in retirement].
Act like the inner young person you have always been.
—J. A. West, writer

Chapter 4
Finding Your Happiness Intersection

Action may not always bring happiness;
but there is no happiness without action.
—Benjamin Disraeli, statesman

At various points in your career, you probably developed a career plan, if for no other reason than you wanted to be able to answer the question: "Where do I want to be in five years?" Over the course of your life, you may have paused and taken another look at where you wanted to go next. Yet, all too often, retirement feels like an ending, not a beginning, and thus not worthy of a plan. In the past, when you only had a few, poor-quality years left, you didn't need a plan. But we know better. We know we're looking at another 30+ years. That's a long time to simply drift. And yet, some people do. There's nothing that will shorten your life so much as letting it just 'happen.'

Morgan couldn't wait till he could retire. Initially, he had loved being a police officer. Following in the footsteps of his father and grandfather, he had no other mission than to be part of the "blue line." His sister also felt the passion and joined the force, though she later left to go to law school and play the safer, more lucrative game. For years, the job had satisfied his need to make a difference and also made it possible for him to provide for his family. At 59, the work had become stale and, frankly, too dangerous as his Los Angeles community began to be overrun with gangs. Morgan saw no future; he'd never been able to pass the detective exam and move up. He never got around to applying to another force, even as the streets became less safe. Friends had started to leave, preferring to retire elsewhere. For years, his wife, Sharleen, pled with him to find a job in a quieter community, somewhere where a loud bang in the night meant a car had backfired, not gunfire.

A year before retirement, he had been shot in a gang shootout and had to "ride a desk" for the last few months. All he wanted to do now was hang up his uniform and walk away from the long hours, the unrewarding pay and the hateful looks on the faces of the people he served.

With the children grown and on their own, he dreamed of a chance to get to really know his wife again. They never had time to travel or even just to sit for hours over dinner, sipping wine together. Too many late night call-outs had made that impossible.

Still, a month into his retirement, he found the days melting together. The couple made no plans, though they talked about doing something. His idea of travel didn't mesh with Sharleen's. She thought of inns and condos; he fantasized about RVing to the national parks. She wanted to move away from Los Angeles; he couldn't summon the energy. He became more sedentary, finding pleasure solely in the meals they shared. But Sharleen had things she wanted to do and, increasingly, Morgan sat at home alone, the blinking eye of the television his only companion. Neither had ever talked about their retirement dreams, and now they were faced with a serious disconnect.

Morgan expected that retirement would just happen, that he would find himself enjoying his time away from work. But he had no plan and no real idea of what he wanted. Still, he was clear on what he didn't want. Knowing what you want can be surprisingly elusive. We think in vague terms about "freedom" without considering what that would look like for us. But it's never too late to start, even for Morgan.

But we've been here before. Remember those long summers away from school, where, initially, the sun didn't stay up long enough to get through the games you played with your friends. Or the one week at camp and other summer activities that you looked forward to through the long school year. Still, by August, days would dawn where you had no thought of what to do. Only the knowledge that your mother would find things for you to do if you couldn't figure it out on your own got you going in the morning. You didn't have a plan, and secretly wished school would come around again to give shape to your life.

Our jobs were like school, shaping each day. We only had to fill in the small spaces with other activities and, as we got older, the responsibilities of a house and children shoved out playtime. We never had to think – What will I do today? More likely, the question would be – What won't I get done? But now, empty hours stretch ahead with no reprieve. As worker bees, we valued our summers off and our vacations because they were rare, precious moments where we could do what we wanted, knowing we had to return to our real lives too soon. Retirement is different. Unless you plan, it's a summer off that never ends and mom is no longer there to relieve your boredom by sending you off with a list of chores. Sure, there's still work you need to do to keep up your house and feed yourself, but that still leaves too many free hours.

We need to plan our later years as we planned our careers; the "Happiness Intersection" is the tool we can use to create our plan. Planning doesn't begin with a 'bucket list' or a travel guide. It starts inside. For perhaps the first time in your life, you're going to focus in on your "wants," the things you enjoy and are good at. Many of us were discouraged from doing this, even at the onset of our careers.

I always knew I could write. In school, getting a writing assignment felt almost as good as recess. Once inspired, the words flowed quickly. Watching my friends gnash their teeth over writing balanced out my struggles with math. In high school, I began entering contests and learning what it takes to become a real writer. But my mother became concerned.

"It's very hard to make a living as a writer," she said. "Even some of the greats never made money on their writing till after they died."

I heeded her words, putting writing aside to focus on another career. But, like a stubborn plant pushing up through lifeless soil demanding to be noticed, my muse would not be ignored. In IT jobs, I found myself documenting procedures and policies, so soon began working on a book while in tedious staff meetings. Katherine Neville, a former bank executive, had paved the way for me, writing her first book at the same company I worked for. When I began to work for software companies, my writing netted me a marketing job that allowed me to write full-time, penning white papers, press releases, blogs and web content. My fellow marketers loved it when I grabbed those assignments; writing wasn't their forte.

Along the way, I sold some work and wrote a novel, "Lifestorm," about the Oakland Hills Firestorm in 1991. In my 50's, I obtained my coaching certificate and began coaching and developing my own model to help people work through transitions. After two layoffs, I applied that model to myself, recognizing that writing had to be a focal point for my life. I wrote three books in three years, thrilling at the feeling of being in my "zone." And, true to my coaching purpose, these books were non-fiction, largely written to share my knowledge of career planning with my friends and colleagues.

Pondering retirement and trying to determine my next steps, I again used my model, the "Happiness Intersection," to reveal my two goals: writing and coaching. This book is the first result of my introspection.

We're told all our lives to focus on what we're good at, but no one mentions that we should also love it. If you were to list everything you did well, the list would be surprisingly long. Yet if you went back and circled the things you still loved to do, you'd find the list would shrink. Throughout your life, the things you are good at and love might change, but it's that intersection that matters. It isn't enough to be good at it; when you also love what you do, this is when you can soar to your greatest heights. For some reason, this element too often is missed in both career and retirement discussions. Before you start making plans, take some time to figure out what you love to do and then how you can get going doing it.

To find your "Happiness Intersection" at any time for yourself, start listing everything you're good at. Take a few days to get a full list, and consult with friends and family – some of us are way too modest and will miss some important items. List everything, even if you can't imagine doing it now. The seeds of your next steps will be found in this list. After you have it completed, spend some time circling the things you love to do now and make a new list of just these items. This exercise helps you begin the vital planning necessary for the rest of your life, whether you plan to work or simply to play.

The secret is that, when you have identified these items, most of what you do next is going to be play. You may choose to earn money or not, go out to volunteer or not, but by understanding what you actually should be doing – your life purpose now – you'll find yourself much happier and feel that your life has meaning.

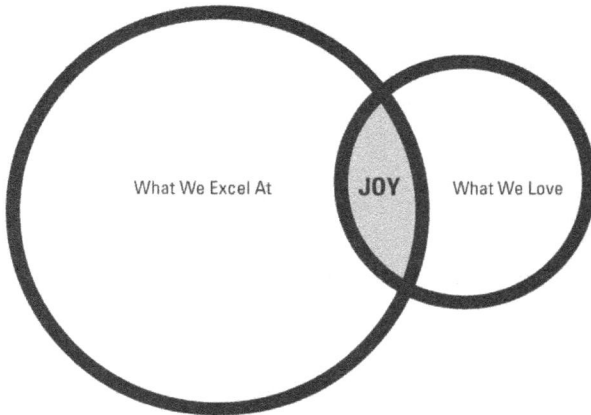

Fig 2. The Happiness Intersection

We could have been doing this our whole lives, but only too often, obligation supersedes joy. We don't have to make that choice anymore. This exercise will help you begin the planning for how you want to spend your time. Without it, your retirement journey will most likely include some spontaneous successes and pleasures, but think of how much more of each you could have when you know what will reap you the most significant rewards. Shouldn't life be fun now?

In the next chapter, we'll start looking at what this means as you figure out how to map the days of your life. With the right base in place – the information you need to understand before you make plans – you have a much higher likelihood of being able to look back on the retirement years as the best years of your life, not a slow slide into old age. We can do better than that.

The happiness of a man in this life does not consist
in the absence but in the mastery of his passions.
—Alfred Lord Tennyson, writer

Chapter 5

Aligning with Your Values

*It's not hard to make decisions when
you know what your values are.*
—Roy Disney, co-founder, Walt Disney Co.

While the Happiness Intersection helps you see a wide range of possibilities, by itself it usually isn't enough to guide your plan. As we age, many of us begin to consider our legacy, our place in the world. Finding meaning in your life may be more important to you now than earlier in your life, when you might have struggled to make ends meet, keep your job, or wrangle with your children.

Looking back at Maslow's Hierarchy of Needs in Chapter 3, esteem and self-actualization are at the peak of the pyramid, aspirational goals when all the others are satisfied. We may find ourselves increasingly concerned about our moral values and obtaining the respect of others as well as respecting ourselves.

In coaching, I often spur this conversation with a question: "What would you want your surviving family and friends to say about you at your funeral?" Another way to ask is, "If you knew you only had six months to live, how would you spend it?" It invites a deeper dive into what truly matters to you now. The answer may differ at various points in our lives.

Devorah felt incredible pride in her son. David, a noted pediatric surgeon, had saved the lives of so many in New York. Furthermore, one month a year David shared his gifts by traveling the world with Doctors Without Borders. Devorah often wondered if that month meant more to him than the rest of the year. His joy bubbled over as he described fixing cleft palates and saving lives with needed surgeries.

"David's always wanted his life to matter," she said, smiling at her best friend, Bev. "Aside from raising him, I wonder what matters about my life."

"Devorah, you're a good person," Bev said. "You're always baking for our temple fund-raisers, and for years the neighborhood relied on you as our backup baby-sitter."

"Yes, but ... don't forget Ruth. I haven't."

Coffee cooled and the conversation lagged as they each retraced their memories of Ruth. Devorah's older child had struggled at every age. Tantrums became rages and violence. Dropping out at 13, she replaced her family with the anodyne of drugs. Long ago, she had disappeared into a new identity; no one had been able to track down Devorah's lost child.

"Maybe you couldn't save her. Perhaps no one could. But what could you do now for someone else?"

Devorah smiled. Bev had always had a knack for the right words at the moment she needed to hear them.

"Something with kids at risk?"

"It's a good place to start. Boys & Girls of America would love your help. There are a lot of great options if you're willing to help children."

Aside from the joyful exploration of travel, hobbies, sports, and other pleasurable retirement activities, part of your retirement time might be spent making meaning in others' lives. To discover what this looks like for you, taking a Values Inventory Test can be very helpful (see Appendix D). Start with your Happiness Intersection list as a way to look at where you can add the most value, then use the results of the Values test to validate each idea. Making sure you live your values is a great way to ensure that your plans satisfy your heart and spirit as well as your mind.

As you take the test, be sure to follow the directions to go with your gut. Don't ponder each answer or you might answer the way you think you should rather than how you really feel. My latest run through the values inventory resulted in discovering that achievement, creativity, independence and responsibility led all others as core values for me now. While I might wish to have higher scores on some values, I have to embrace who I am. I suspect all of us can remember at least one time in our life when we tried to be someone we weren't. I remember when I wanted to be the popular girl in junior high school. I carefully replicated the behavior of the cool girls, and initially it succeeded. Boys were more interested in me. The trouble was I couldn't maintain this fake persona. Worse, I didn't really respect these guys; they didn't really want me. I wasn't living my values.

When you embrace a life value that you think you should have rather than those you really feel, the result of your efforts is often unrewarding.

Simon had carved out his 'success path' from his early days. An avid student, he aced every class and got early acceptance from several prestigious schools. Law schools begged him to choose their offer; he happily accepted Harvard's bid. After graduation, he had his choice of prestigious firms from which to begin his career. He chose a prominent firm in Kentucky, enjoying the lush, green valleys. Later in life, he married a gorgeous actress, had the requisite two children, and upgraded cars and houses with each step of his career. He made his fortune representing companies that were being sued by consumers, such as several of the more prominent cigarette manufacturers.

One day, a friend from college visited him at his summer

home in Vero Beach. Jack whistled, admiring the spacious beachfront "cottage." Selecting one of a wide choice of hard-to-find beers at the pool fridge, Jack said, "I have to ask. Are you happy?"

Simon snorted. "Are you kidding me? I've got it all. Just look around."

"What I see is a man who looks decades older than me, whose smile hasn't shown up since I arrived, and whose wife and kids aren't around to meet me."

"Yeah, well." Simon tried a grin, noting the difficulty he had in maintaining it. "It's all good. It's everything I ever dreamed about."

"Then why aren't you happy? Looks like a mid-life crisis to me, even though you managed to save it till you were 60."

"Gina left me. Took the kids. Thank God for the pre-nup or I would have been screwed over. Still, I had to pay out for the kids," Simon muttered. He didn't like the taste of his words.

"You always had it planned out. I envied that. You knew what you wanted, right? I had to figure it out, over time."

"But now you know?"

"Sure. But first I had to give up trying to impress everyone around me. I realized that all I wanted was to impress myself and the people who mattered. And what impresses my kids is being around for their lives. I couldn't work the hours that netted the big bucks, but I realized I would never get back their childhood. My wife needed me around too."

"So, life is good?"

Jack smiled. "Almost without realizing it and without the detailed plan you had, I got everything I ever wanted in life. But it took knowing what I wanted, not what other people thought I should want."

"Going to retire?"

"Soon. We need a few more years in, so I can do what I really want when I give up my firm. I'm going to just do the cases that really matter to me, pro-bono. We'll stay in Kansas. We can afford to retire there."

Simon took a deep breath. "I'm not sure what I really want anymore. This is all stuff. I have more money than I can spend and nothing I care about. I wonder…. Can you stay a few days and help me figure out what's next for me? You seem to have a better plan than I have."

It's so easy to get caught up believing in someone else's cultural values rather than our own. How many of us strove to climb the ladder even when the job we already had really reflected the job we most wanted to do? I watched many people sacrifice their lives to get the next promotion. For some, the choice cost them their family. For others, it took them from doing what they enjoyed and were good at to doing work they hated. In cases like this, it's easy for the "Impostor Syndrome" to set in. While I sometimes felt torn, wondering if I should work more towards promotions and dollars than focus on what I enjoyed, I realized that this wouldn't be worth it. Becoming a CEO may be someone else's dream. We have to live our own.

When we match up our dreams and values, not only are we more satisfied with our lives, we also find we don't waste money or time. Remember the concept of "keeping up with the Joneses?" Ever feel pressured to do something or buy something because everyone else values these things? We've all done it, but once we track to what we really want and value, every minute and every dollar is invested in those values. It's never wasted. For me, shopping is a chore, and increasingly I find I don't want a lot of things. But money spent on travel is money well spent; I get so much from meeting new people, discovering new cultures and learning about new cuisines. And, I've found work I love, so I plan to keep working until that is no longer true for me.

At this point in our lives, we have less time left than we

have already lived. We've also spent a lot of our time raising families, earning a living, and often doing what we needed to do rather than what we wanted. Get clear on your values and your next steps become clear.

Chapter 6

Mining Your Bucket List

*I don't want to get to the end of my life and find
that I lived just the length of it.
I want to have lived the width of it as well.*
—Diane Ackerman, poet and essayist

Got a bucket list? While few of us have a physical list, most of us have some dreams that as yet haven't been realized. Life has a way of getting in the way of dreams unless we make a point of taking control of our time. When we say goodbye to our 60+ hour a week job, we should also say goodbye to excuses. Start looking at those activities and adventures you've deferred before you no longer have the physical capacity to enjoy them. Our aging bodies may eliminate options; sooner is always better to spill some of your must-do items from the bucket.

Years ago, I began to realize the importance of this, of investing in experiences even if it meant a small hit to the retirement investments I could make. Waiting made no sense if I could manage to do it when I wanted to and was able to. I took a few cruises, went sky-diving, learned to scuba and ran races. I was taking advantage of all that life had to offer. One of my neighbors helped to inspire me. This quiet gentleman had worked his entire life and saved carefully for his retirement. At one point, he shared his plans with me, commenting that he didn't feel all that well, but hoped to be better for the big party his company threw for him. A few weeks later, he learned he had cancer of the heart, a death sentence. He lasted another month, his plans unrealized, his retirement dreams shattered. Life is fickle; you never know when what you rely on will be taken away.

In grad school, we all admired one of the PhD candidates who spent all his free time training for races and traveling to run them. He constantly challenged his personal best and worked to achieve Olympic-level fitness while still finding the time to enjoy himself. Most of the rest of us spent too many hours in the lab; hiking up hills to the medical campus and then to the main campus constituted "exercise." I had a group of friends with whom I played volleyball, followed by a run to a bar for pitchers of beer. In the summer, the same group did some sailing at Baseline Lake. We relished the breaks we carved out of our schedules, but also felt guilty. We were there to build our career profiles, not to have a great time.

Our PhD friend finished and landed a post-doc in a neighboring state. In the first year, we learned he had died of an undetected heart condition while training. A few of us panicked and checked in for comprehensive physicals. The rest of us acknowledged how short life can be and made a further commitment to live it.

Turning your desires into reality can be a great source of joy, but it is fraught with peril. If you have always wanted to scale the Matterhorn, you probably can't defer this goal until you're 70. But most of us are already at a point where some plans no longer make sense. You need to go deeper and find what really matters to you at this point in life, tempered by what you can actually accomplish.

It can help to ask some questions of yourself as you consider the things you want to do. Sadly, some ambitions may have become impossibilities. But many may still be possible.

Why do I want to do it? This question helps you unpack your assumptions about the idea as well as what you hope to achieve.

How would I do it? If you hate to fly or travel by boat, some places and dreams will be beyond reach. Consider your fitness level and abilities. Scaling a mountain requires training, endurance and strength. However, you can ride a gondola to the top of many mountains if your passion is to see the top of the world and enjoy the vistas. Research options. SNUBA is easier and more accessible than scuba. Figure out if there is a way to do something you want, even if it isn't your first-choice method.

Am I able to do it? Sky-diving may be your dream, but many facilities won't take someone with back problems or heart issues. Other plans may require training.

What do I feel inside when I think about this idea? Check out your emotions; this isn't simply an intellectual exercise.

What are the logistics? Do the research and prepare a detailed plan. This is when you discover limitations such as needing special visas or permits to travel, training to accomplish the activity, or possibly other restrictions.

What you loved when you were young may not give you the same thrill as you get older. I wanted to have a motorcycle even as late as my early '50s. Now, I have absolutely no interest in even riding one, though I probably wouldn't say no to a one-time experience. I'm thrilled I did the fun ocean cruises in the Caribbean when I was young. Now, the idea of the more sedate and peaceful European river cruises appeals more.

Consider all kinds of crazy options. Take a painting class. Read a book you've always meant to read. Take up a new sport or an instrument. So much of this time is about expanding your horizons to new possibilities. At this point, we're not locked into things. Run/walk the Bay to Breakers or another organized "fun run." Go zip-lining, even if it scares you. You never know what you might enjoy until you give it a whirl. Have fun with the exercise.

One fun way to start is look up activities on deal sites like Groupon or TravelZoo. Grab a friend or your spouse and try something out. Join a book club and be prepared to read someone else's selection. Even when it goes horribly wrong (like having to read "50 Shades of Gray"), the discussions will be hysterical. Browse Meetup.com and find a new group to join.

And to really hit your core "musts," ask yourself the question—If I had six months to live (and had my health), what would I do with those last days? The question can really focus your mind.

Over the years of meeting obligations and doing what other people want, we might forget that we had our own hopes and ambitions, so many of which never got met. At best, retirement is about nothing more than getting up every day to do what we want to do. Let's go figure it out and get started.

Chapter 7

Traveling Well

Why do you go away? So that you can come back.
So that you can see the place you came from
with new eyes and extra colors.
And the people there see you differently, too.
Coming back to where you started
is not the same as never leaving.
—Terry Pratchett, writer

Many of us want to prioritize travel now that we don't have to cram it into two or three weeks of vacation. We have the luxury of time and a world to explore. Many experiences can be enjoyed well into our later years, particularly if we take good care of our bodies. But others may be experienced now. If you don't plan, you may find that a travel adventure you only thought about earlier in life may be impossible now. For some types of travel, it may already be too late, but consider alternatives that might work. While you may not be able to hike as you once did, you might be able to rent an ATV or join a group driving to otherwise inaccessible spots. You need to go deeper and find what really matters to you at this point in life, tempered by what you can actually accomplish and prioritized by the degree of fitness required.

I started traveling young, beginning with moving to Ann Arbor for grad school and enjoying a Pleasant Hawaiian Holiday to Oahu a few years later. Going on my first ocean cruise in my 20s, I saw elderly people struggling to get around. Each doorway had a riser, presumably to help seal off areas of the ship in a disaster, but those few inches spelled immobility for many. The gangplank and pool area represented a challenge, and I rarely saw these people enjoying the active shore excursions offered. I made a vow not to wait. Still, there are plenty of undiscovered ideas left in my dream bucket. It's time to get started.

As with any investment, it pays to do some research to determine the value to you of a particular kind of itinerary. What do you enjoy doing when you travel? What kinds of accommodations do you prefer? What parts of the world attract you most? And – very important – what is the optimal amount of time you'd like to be away? Take the time to do your homework. Many dreams shipwreck when you finally take them out to sea.

Martin and Lisa envied their friends, Gennady and Sybil. Days after retiring, the couple rented their out their Dallas house and took off on a two-year adventure of non-stop traveling, which included renting a sailboat for a few months of touring the Caribbean. Instagram updates whetted Martin and Lisa's appetite to see the world. They had been to so few places, too caught up in making sure the kids had the requisite Disney trips as well as visiting the in-laws regularly.

Gennady invited them to stay at their rented villa in Positano for a few weeks. Excited to get started, they booked a plane to Rome, planning to see some of the north first before joining their friends. For two weeks, they moved from city to city, trying to cram in the sights, while regretting that they hadn't spent more time studying the guidebooks they had with them. It proved difficult to find restaurants that could address their diverse diet needs; Martin had to watch his cholesterol and Lisa wanted to avoid gluten, a tough challenge in a land founded on pasta and with menus printed in Italian.

By the time they boarded the train to Positano, Martin and

Lisa realized they missed being home. Lisa loved to cook and became tired of restaurant fare. Martin enjoyed the historic treasures in each city, but realized he might have preferred to just spend a week in Rome and not move around so much. Inexperienced, they both had brought too much luggage.

Gennady showed up at the train station to greet them in a Fiat, a car too small to take both of them and their bags. They ordered a cab, again regretting the desire to be "ready for anything." They enjoyed seeing their friends and driving around the area, but after a few days, Lisa admitted to Martin that she was bored. And neither of them expected the narrow streets and hilly nature of the town. The amount of walking required put a big strain on their knees. Neither felt comfortable with any form of public transit, an option they had rarely used anywhere.

"I guess I'd rather sit by the pool and drink wine at home," she confessed.

Both looked forward to getting back and rethinking their travel reveries.

Get a bunch of your friends in a room together to share their favorite travel stories. As the details emerge, you might notice the most striking aspect is how each person defines having a great time. While some may love RVing and camping, others need a luxury hotel to really feel pampered. Still others enjoy the feeling of being a local by staying in unusual AirBnB's or VRBOs. A few still love the open road. After years of horrible commutes, others prefer being driven or flown around.

Understand why you wish to travel. When you return, what will you have learned, experienced and discovered? When you know the why, a lot of the details become much clearer.

Make some notes on places you want to see, and then go deeper. How will you get there? What kind of accommodations do you prefer? How expensive is the destination, and is there a way to do it more economically? If it's a popular site, how do you feel about competing with crowds? Research will show you ways to "skip the line," even at venues like the Louvre or the Uffizi.

Many people have always wanted to travel by sea, but questions abound here. What size of ship do you like? Many ports, or few? Mostly adult, or family-friendly? It's worth finding a great travel professional (some of us have more than one with expertise in specific areas). To avoid disappointment, do your homework and really consider what you like and what turns you off. I once dreamed of attending Oktoberfest in Munich ... until I saw the vast setup and started considering what a mob scene it would be. Being a reasonably light drinker, the immense beer steins would have knocked me for a loop and made navigating the many tents and events even more difficult. I ended up relishing hitting a few beer halls, trying one smaller beer at a time while enjoying the relative peace of places like the Hofbräuhaus off-season.

When you know what attractions are offered in a place, you can more easily pick a season. Outdoor activities are challenging when it's rainy or cold. Weather is flaky, so be prepared with clothing and alternative plans for any eventuality. Even when you've checked the weather right before you leave, as anything can happen. But you'll be happier choosing the season that best matches what you want to do. A museum-focused vacation could work well at any time of the year, though the hours open may be more limited. But if you're a nature-hound, you'll want weather that allows you to enjoy the beauty you seek. Even Alaska-bound travelers need to consider what they want to see and when. The days are very short in the winter and yet, if you struggle to sleep without light cues, the summer days are endless.

Check out options such as the HopOn/HopOff buses and boats and public transportation cards available in many places.

Getting around can get expensive, even with Uber, and public transit can not only save you a bundle, but also allow you to be part of the community. Online sites in English help make this easy. In some cases, the tourist public transportation cards may offer you discounts to highly valued attractions as well.

The good news is that travel planning is much easier now. You can tour hotel rooms on the Internet, as well as checking out maps, distances, travel times, and much more. I've found it very helpful to study a physical travel book or two when I plan; they are available at libraries, and I often even buy one to take along. These books can be incredibly valuable if anything goes wrong; they always list hospitals and other helpful information. After reviewing a few library offerings, you can figure out whose guidance you prefer and which fits your travel style. To save weight, print out or photocopy the most helpful pages.

These books (and many online guides) will also help you prepare to deal with crowds better. Before the Internet, we went to Florence intending to hit the major museums. A travel guide told me to call a few numbers in Italy to pre-book entry. It cost a foreign phone call (more expensive back then) and a few dollars per ticket, but was well worth it. Arriving at the Uffizi, we saw a line stretching along the entire interior courtyard. I saw a ticket office, presented my tickets, and bypassed the line. I later learned they only allow a certain small number in at any time, so those without a reservation waited until we finished our tour. Even as retirees, time is still precious. No one travels to spend time in line.

Don't assume that nothing will have changed, even at a site you've been to before. On a recent trip to Amsterdam, I had a last-minute thought that perhaps the Van Gogh and Rijksmuseum might be busier than a trip I took in 2004. Back then, you could walk into either without difficulty. At 2AM, the night before we left, I went online and booked tickets for both. (No, I don't sleep well before a trip; there's always something left to do.) When we arrived, our pre-planning paid off. Not only did we see huge lines at both venues, but the Van Gogh required a cash payment, and not everyone had bothered to exchange enough money.

While many take off expecting to use credit cards everywhere, you may find that doesn't work, especially in smaller towns. You'll need a debit card with a chip AND a PIN to use ATMs and many ticket machines. You'll also want to carry some cash. Few buses take cards and those delightful cafes and craft fairs only take cash. In most cities, you'll find a bank ATM you can use to resupply. Don't miss a great opportunity because you haven't planned.

Check visa rules and your passport date. If only six months remain on your passport, get it updated. Also check EU rules if you travel there. While most of the EU allowed Americans to travel anywhere in the Schengen zone without a check after being scanned at the first entry point, the rules are changing.

Keep up on your chargers. For most devices, basic adapters will work, but some European countries recently added a new feature, one that ensures older adaptors don't work. Besides, you'll want ones that include USB ports as well; it's much easier to charge this way. Carry your electronics, adaptors, cords, passport, credit cards and any needed drugs in your carry-on. Everyone has lost luggage; you need to be able to survive a day or two without it. On that note, a valuable trick is to not only put your travel itinerary and contact info into your checked luggage; also get a luggage tag that allows you to insert a copy outside the bag. You can find one that tells the reader what's inside in many different languages. You don't check your bags? Guess again. Many places outside the US have very tight rules regarding luggage. The normal mega-roller you can sling onto a Southwest flight may just be too big or too heavy for EasyJet.

Does this all sound like too much work? In fact, it can be fun. Once you have a plan of action listing the activities you need to do to ensure a great trip, AND you give yourself enough time to plan, you'll find the payoff when you actually arrive. My detailed planning meant I could give into spontaneous activities like having a drink and a free concert on Piazza San Marco or saving big money checking my bags by pre-paying the luggage fee. As you travel more, you'll learn the tips and tricks that save your vacation.

While many of us poke fun at visitors to our towns who take a tour bus, such a tour can provide you a great overview of the layout where you're visiting. It's also a great way to get tips on wonderful restaurants, little known haunts you really would regret missing, and much more. Years ago, turned on by a tip from a local, I started hitting up neighborhood groceries while traveling. I met locals, learned a great deal about their food culture, created some low-cost, delicious picnics, and found better gifts to bring back to friends and family.

You never know how travel will change you if you open yourself to the possibilities.

After a layoff, Navya traveled to Rome from her Kansas City home, wanting to get away from all the reminders of her job, a position that had never thrilled her. For fun, she had added Italian to her language base, which included Hindi and Tamil. After a week, she discovered people in smaller towns who wished to learn English. She found a way to earn enough to stay longer by working at a school for adults.

For years, friends had encouraged to try to get some singing gigs. Her rich and mellow voice had carried her through high school musicals and chorus. She loved singing, but never seriously considered it as a career. One night, sitting down with new Italian friends at a taverna, she mentioned her love of singing.

Shortly after, they got the band to invite her up for a song. The taverna owner hired her on the spot. Between the language lessons and the singing, Navya stayed for a year, turning a short vacation into a new lifestyle.

While not everyone will make a move like this, some discover a second home on their tour. Being part of the town can be a wonderful and very different experience than simply visiting.

Travelling the world pays off in so many ways. It's one of the powerful ways we can continue our learning, both about others and about ourselves. Even if you never venture outside the US, you can discover different worlds, from the Amish of Pennsylvania to the Acadians of Louisiana. Make travel a part of your retirement adventure.

Chapter 8

To Work … or Not?

Yes, I've made a great deal of dough from my fiction, but I never set a single word down on paper with the thought of being paid for it … I have written because it fulfilled me. Maybe it paid off the mortgage on the house and got the kids through college, but those things were on the side—I did it for the buzz. I did it for the pure joy of the thing. And if you can do it for the joy, you can do it forever.
—Stephen King, writer

To work or not to work goes to the heart of the retirement re-definition. Many people love their jobs; few are forced out now because of age, though it can happen with some professions. If you love what you're doing now, you have some options. More companies are offering older employees the chance to work a reduced schedule. This can be a great way to ease out of the 40+ hour grind and reduce commute days. Others will consider work-from-home options to keep you onboard. The more valuable you are, the more options you will find. In most cases, you'll need to raise the issue. Not every manager is familiar with these programs. It's a great idea to consider these before pulling the plug on your career if you're still having fun.

A Texas native, Levar had worked for 40 years for the same company, rising from an operator position to his current role as a senior IT architect. As he reached his 65th birthday, his wife and friends encouraged him to take a package; the company sought to cut its numbers and offered nice options for those who would leave. For people his age, they offered a small pension, severance pay, and even unemployment benefits. COBRA was an option as well. Levar couldn't refuse this good of a package, even as he wondered what he would do with his time.

His wife, Nia, welcomed him home. She had retired a year earlier and loved working in her garden, taking short walks and spending time with their grandchildren. The home they had bought outside of Austin turned out to be the perfect location and size, so she felt no pressure to move. Levar knew she had a honey-do list waiting for him: things they both wanted to do around the house to make it more comfortable. Still, after a day of hammering, he didn't feel the same satisfaction as he got from solving a tough project at work. They traveled a bit, but he found himself missing work.

After a few months, he managed to find another job and relaxed back into his old routine. Nia missed having him at home, but she didn't miss his disgruntlement. Levar needed to work. He had no other interest that fulfilled or satisfied him as much as the job he had.

Like Stephen King, Levar had found his life's "sweet spot" with his career. Family pressure, friends' expectations, and the onset of aging can make you feel like it's just time to go. But retiring from your career isn't the right answer for everyone. Consider this issue before you make a decision. It can be much more difficult to get rehired when you're older.

Life without choices can be even more complex. Airline pilots are retired when they hit 65 (only a short time back, the age was 60). For so many, flying has always been the job of their dreams, a life passion. With no choice, malaise and depression can ensue.

Rich loved flying so much that even as a child, he saved every cent for flying lessons. After his college graduation, he

signed up with the Air Force, knowing that having this experience could virtually guarantee him an aviation career. Muster-
ing out, he joined the airlines. He flew extra flights, seeing no
reason to be home when he could be in the cockpit. Although
San Francisco had been his final base, he rarely had time to experience it. On his 65th birthday, he ignored the pleas of friends
and family to celebrate with them. Instead, he rented a single-
engine Cessna and flew to Half Moon Bay for a solitary seafood
lunch at Barbara's Fishtrap. While he enjoyed the coastal views,
the minimal challenges of flying a small plane and the "$100
hamburger" left him feeling bereft. None of it mattered.

If you love flying, your choices are limited. The age cap is
an FAA mandate, but there's a way around it, a way to make a
difference. A friend told him about the volunteer opportunities
available for pilots and forwarded the following URL:
http://www.volunteerpilots.net/organizations/   While some
agencies require the pilot to donate his time and a plane, not
all do. He found several agencies in California and immediately
signed up.

"At least they don't care so much about age," he said.

Finding a new way to continue your profession when you
no longer need the large paycheck can be a great option.
When we love what we do but have the means to support ourselves, giving back may be the right move for you. For many
of us, the challenge will be to find a volunteer opportunity that
challenges us, makes us feel useful, and rewards us by making
a difference. Too many charities and non-profits want to save
the interesting jobs for paid employees (why?) and save the
menial work for volunteers. But this may be changing. Figure
out what you'd enjoy and how you can contribute, then get
the word out there.

Some people are tired of doing what they had been doing
and long for something new. If you're like them, you may find

that completely retiring isn't enough. Just because you no longer like the work you've been doing doesn't mean that you need to stop working. Experts believe that millennials will change careers many times during their lives. We live too long and are too healthy in our later years to stop growing and learning. What have you always wanted to do? What do you do well and love? Go back to the Happiness Intersection and consider new careers by using that tool. If you've got enough money saved up, you can take a job you love even if it doesn't provide the six-figure income you may have had previously.

Burnout can take years off your life, and long commutes and the stress they cause impact your immune system. We deserve to be happy now, and what makes us happy may still be work. Years ago, I took a communications class from a gentleman who was a gifted speaker. He shared with us that he had been an MD until he turned 50 and decided he needed something completely different. He gave up medicine, a surprising choice, but one he felt had to make. You could hear the passion and energy in his voice.

Some clients have worked with me to put their talents to use at a non-profit. No longer needing the higher salary, they want to work on a program that inspires passion for them. You have choices.

While starting this book, I considered what to do with my business. Some clients had disappeared, while my coaching workload had increased. What does retirement mean to the self-employed? I came to the realization that "retirement" is just a word; if I wanted to call myself retired, I could. I needed to ignore the way others saw the word; I could craft my own definition. When my Medicare card arrived, I decided to call my 65th birthday retirement day. I'm doing exactly what I want to be doing and enjoying my life more than ever, while almost nothing has changed. The operative word for me was "choice." Everything I do now (besides the inevitable hassles of chores and the like) will be what I want to do.

A few of you may have to work. The most careful saver and planner can still be faced with unexpected financial challenges requiring your work life to continue. While money may be the main object, don't forget to look for where your abilities and passions align. Not only will you enjoy the work a great deal more, you'll also excel at it and stand out for your contribution. When we play in our Happiness Intersection, no one can beat us. And "work" can stop being a four-letter work.

If you're brave enough to say goodbye,
life will reward you with a new hello.
—Paul Coelho, lyricist and writer

Chapter 9

Volunteering

The best way to find yourself
is to lose yourself in the service of others.
—Mahatma Gandhi

Finding meaning in your life can often become even more important as we get older. If your day job didn't make you feel like you had moved the needle on helping others, retirement might be a time when volunteering becomes a bigger part of your life. The challenge is to find a volunteer position that takes advantage of your unique skills and interests.

Terri had successfully launched her kids through college and into great careers. Tired of the endless chores in maintaining the family home in Minneapolis, she relocated to a condo in a 55+ community in Tucson, a place she had always loved to visit. With family a plane ride away and house chores minimal, she found herself bored too much of the time. Even with all the planned activities, she didn't find enough motivation to wake up and get going each day.

As a nurse, every day had brought a feeling that her work mattered. Her last years working in a chemotherapy unit had been particularly rewarding. Terri loved the chance to help people stay positive and strong through their treatments and loved leading a support group to help women navigate life after mastectomies. She remembered how much she enjoyed Candy Striping when a teen; it inspired her career. Still, she thought she might be a bit old for the pink and white costume.

Talking with the Activities director at her complex, Terri learned that some of the older residents had a serious challenge, one she could definitely solve. Single retirees often found meeting with a doctor very challenging, particularly when they received bad news. As she knew all too well, once your doctor tells you that you have a serious illness or problem, your mind shuts off.

"You don't hear what they say. All you can do is panic," she said.

The director nodded. "I wonder if you would be willing to go with some of them to their appointments. You could take notes and ask the right questions, then help them understand options and outcomes."

The idea of becoming a patient advocate inspired Terri. She quickly found herself a role, one that got her jumping out of bed each morning. As time went on, she began working with the director to organize support groups as well. One day, she realized how crammed her calendar had become, but she loved every minute of it.

Terri's volunteer choice met several important criteria. First, it stemmed from her expertise. She knew how to help people in this way. Second, it filled her heart. Every day, she knew she had made a difference for someone. Third, she enjoyed the challenge of demystifying "medicalese." Finally, she made many new friends, adding to her daily joy.

Just like Rich in the last chapter, the best volunteer opportunities stem from your Happiness Intersection, doing something you love and are good at. One challenge is finding the right position. Often, like Terri, you have to create your own role. One of my friends loved her IT job, but when she retired, ran into the problem of where she could make a contribution. After some discussion, it turned out she had a strong artistic flair as well as great IT skills. Deciding she could make incredible web pages for non-profits, we worked together to figure out which ones really tugged at her heart. She found that almost every charity worried that their site didn't help their fundraising effort. Most had no idea how to really craft a compelling page, but she did. The result was definitely win/win.

While most of us say we're willing to do anything, in fact, almost no one can stand hours of making phone calls or stuffing envelopes. Still, when you achieve clarity on what you want to do, you may find it easier to make a case for a better role. Years ago, I started volunteering with Planned Parenthood. The regular jobs didn't thrill me. Anyone could answer the phone, make appointments and greet patients. With my medical background, I managed to leap into a much more interesting role, that of pregnancy counselor. I ran the tests, reported the results to the client, and together we figured out what she wanted to do. Much like the coaching job I have now, asking good questions and really listening to individual issues made me a valuable resource. And, let's face it, I had a lot more fun doing something that took advantage of what I liked to do and excelled at.

In many states, you will be limited to helping out only non-profits and/or government agencies, constraining your options. In California, it's illegal to have volunteers at for-profit companies, an obscure law that flattened a local winemaker who wanted to share his love of wine with willing retirees. Yes, if you want to pour wine tastes and discuss varietals at a winery in California, they have to pay you. Still, at a minimum wage, it may feel like volunteering, so go for it if you've had a hankering to learn more about wine and love to chat with people.

In some cases, the work you can offer makes more sense when some pay is involved, even if you don't need the money. While training as a coach, I learned that "free coaching" rarely achieved the desired results; most people needed to have some kind of stake in the endeavor.

The fee could be small, but with the exchange of money I could see the degree of commitment increase. My first coaching training was creativity coaching. As the course proceeded, we had clients assigned to us. While initial meetings generally went well, the compliance with assignments fell off with each succeeding meeting. My clients just didn't have an investment in their success. My inexperience contributed to the problem, but I definitely found that having to pay for a service resulted in clients coming prepared and willing to work to achieve their goals.

I should have known this. Years ago, I participated in Project READ. Initially, the work involved reading to 1st graders to get them hooked on books. But with a captive group of adults on hand, the coordinator decided to also assign us struggling second-graders to teach. None of us had the slightest idea of how to teach reading and, sadly, couldn't remember how we learned. Yet, almost every child ended the year reading at grade level despite the lack of expertise on the part of their teachers. And then we learned that each child had volunteered for this program, giving up their lunch once a week to participate. They had skin in the game and wanted to learn.

When I taught in grad school, undergrads funded by their parents didn't tend to work as hard as those paying their own way, nor did they typically graduate in four years. This rule may apply to many of the services you might offer. Be willing to charge a nominal fee just to increase the engagement and cement the value of your work. You can always adjust it for the circumstances.

To figure out the kinds of the work you might do, go back to your Happiness Intersection. Love animals? Animal rescue shelters always need volunteers to work with the animals and help them get adopted. It does mean cleaning out litter and sweeping, but you'll be around your favorite animals. My cherished rabbit rescue groups always need people to show rabbits at pet stores to help inspire adoptions. Knowledge of the animal(s) you might work with makes all the difference. New animal parents need your insights and experience. Into politics? Candidates always need help, and often will let experienced volunteers do interesting things such as help with speech writing.

Part of my struggle with the idea of retirement was figuring out a volunteer challenge I would enjoy. Despite a long, rewarding IT career, I wanted nothing more to do with it. I loved coaching, but knew that for most, paying something made a difference in the result. My husband gave me an idea that is now my passion project—coaching veterans on starting their post-military careers. I remembered dating a Vietnam era vet who told me he didn't know what he could do in the "real world."

"I'm great at killing people," he said. "Not something you put on a resume."

I remember thinking, "Why not?" After working with hundreds of coaching clients, I could see that a sniper has a ton of capabilities that make them an excellent fit in the business world. Patience, self-control, leadership, mastery of complex systems, adaptable to rapidly changing scenarios, mission planning, and more. Helping vets get their next job will be an occupation I really want to do; I know how much it will mean to me and how my experience can help them.

In the end, the best opportunities are the ones you create yourself by being crystal clear on the ways you want to help and what you can bring to the table. Check Appendix D for some good links to stimulate your imagination.

As you grow older, you will discover that you have two hands
— one for helping yourself, the other for helping others.
                —Audrey Hepburn, actress

FOCUSING ON
THE DETAILS

Chapter 10

The Importance of Plans, Schedules and Lists

A goal without a plan is just a wish.
—Antoine de Saint-Exupéry, writer and aviator

Whether you used a paper Day-Timer or another planner, or preferred to plan your day on an email server such as Outlook, every work day had a shape. We managed to do our work between interminable meetings, deftly multi-tasking our way to success. Commuters learned how to use smart phones to continue to function even through two-hour commutes. Even weekends—those too-short hours of rest—had lists of must-dos vying for our attention with the more pleasurable activities, as well as sleep. We got a lot done because we had so little time. Without a schedule or plan, bills wouldn't get paid, kids wouldn't get taken to endless rounds of activities, and the house would become a hoarder's dream.

As a retiree, too often we find the hours slipping away. Part of the allure of retirement seems to be the freedom from schedules, but that freedom comes with a price. Without a plan, how do you prioritize and get things done?

Vilma slept until 8AM the first two weeks after leaving her sales consultant job. All the years of waking at 4 to get everyone ready to go so she could hit the road before the awful logjam on the 405 started had made her rebel against her alarm. Kid-free, and with a husband who used his mental alarm to rise on demand, she described sleeping-in as toe-wriggling good.

Except without all that movement.

Catching up with her still-working friend Tanesha, she confessed she hadn't even done any house-cleaning.

"The dishes get done, but that wouldn't happen if we didn't have a dishwasher," she said. "I can cook more interesting meals now, but find I never seem to get to dusting or vacuuming. Rashid even ran out of clean clothes last week."

"Girlfriend, you always stayed on top of your stuff. What's happening to you now?"

Vilma frowned. "I have no idea. By any measure, I have more time than I ever did, but I get nothing done. I thought this would be a great time. I wanted to do so many things. I had plans."

"Weren't you guys going to finally take that Alaska cruise?"

"I haven't had time to sit down and look at the brochures."

The most precious commodity we have now is time, but because we have so much of it, it can slip from our fingers like sand, never to be recovered. More important, we need to do things while we still have the physical and mental ability to enjoy them. Deferred dreams become impossibilities as the map we play on shrinks. Look at house-bound 90-year-olds, their driver's license a distant memory. Invest time now to take advantage of your freedom.

Dream vacations never turn into actual trips without planning. A successful retirement begins with dreams and ideas, but only becomes reality when you make a plan, define a list of necessary activities, and put it on your schedule. Much like a project, the well-lived life requires planning. Project managers may find this easier than some, but for the rest of us, some tools are necessary. Fortunately, we all have them at hand.

Define the project. No matter what it is, a project deserves a nice manila folder with the project name emblazoned on it.

If you're still working, you'll find tons of barely-used, discarded folders at work. I'm still recycling from that pile myself. For major projects, you may need several folders; each big project deserves a hanging green folder in which all the files can reside. You can get an inexpensive folder box to store all your projects in, making it easy to access them on demand. I have one hanging rack with all my travel plans filed away. I also have a folder for my TSA-Pre paperwork and general travel information, such as changes in visa rules, airport information, and parking information and coupons. A second, general-purpose folder contains travel ideas. These are destinations I might go to at some point, but I haven't begun to plan for as yet.

On the cover of the manila folders for travel, I always attach a Post-it Note, detailing the major items that need to be completed: air travel, airport parking, hotel(s), pet-sitter acquired, etc. Into the folder goes the results of my planning, which might be city maps, transit maps, print-outs of all reservations, etc. For a complex trip, such as the one I have planned for next year, I'll have a few files for each destination: River Cruise, Barcelona, Madrid, Valencia. With this system, I not only ensure everything is completed, I also have clarity on what still needs to be done. For my 65th birthday trip to Chicago, I've included Post-its on my calendar for when to make reservations for dinners and various planned activities. As a result, I have high confidence in a great, well-planned trip, one that I can enjoy planning as well as taking.

While all this planning may sound like it takes spontaneity out of the equation, nothing could be further from the truth. Nothing spells disappointment like coming home and having people ask you how you enjoyed some iconic treasure you never knew existed. You want to know your priorities. There will also be time to play and live in the moment. No one schedules vacations so tightly that there's no time left. Even work travel can give rise to serendipitous adventures. On a trip to Norfolk, VA, I found myself alone, my co-workers stuck with delayed flights from another city. Instead of heading to my room to do email, I asked the hotel desk clerk where I might find a good option for food. He told me about a riverfront festival with food, music and vendor booths taking place that evening. To my delight, not only did I enjoy a fabulous picnic dinner, I ate it while listening to the Neville Brothers work their magic as the sun set on the harbor. I also bought one of my favorite bread cookbooks from a vendor. My co-workers really missed out, but in reality they might have anyway. Locals are great sources of inspiration, but you have to talk to them to learn your options.

But not all your dreams are travel. If you're looking for volunteer opportunities, start collecting information in another file. When I do this, reviewing the file often gives me more ideas. And I can go back to it whenever I wish for more inspiration.

Yes, I had multiple Medicare files (see Appendix A). When I sat down to apply, I had everything where I needed it to be and could make decisions easily and with great confidence. Now, those files have transformed into plan files, highlighting the plan details, my applications, and later my claims. My files made what might be a confusing situation into a no-brainer.

I can imagine the tech-savvy of you thinking: "I have files on my PC. Why do I need paper files?" With 35-plus years in IT, you might imagine me to be paperless. The truth is that paper can save your bacon. Too often, people have problems with their phone, and TSA gate agents have no patience with that. One time, I remember the phone reader didn't work; only paper boarding passes got you on board. I've gotten that last hotel room in an oversell by presenting the paper trail proving my reservation. It sounds so 20th century, but paper really works. I do love apps, just like the next person, but I remember my Paris Metro app not really working right when I actually needed it. Instead, my paper Metro map, tucked away in my travel purse, saved the day.

I'm having my shower redone and, yes, I have a file that keeps track of my communications, as I preferred to delay it until I had more of the payment on hand. I can go back and verify all of the details. Some information came through email; I printed it.

If moving to another location appeals to you, you'll definitely want to track your experiences and feelings as you visit possible locales, as well as the details. A move is complex.

Once you start designing a system, you'll be amazed at how much this kind of thing can help you. Increasing numbers of families find it a dietary challenge to host a holiday meal. Isn't Joe gluten-free? Then there's Darla, with the heart issue; got to watch the fats for her. And Jennifer prefers to eat vegetarian unless salmon is on the menu. Set up a quick party-planner file with a list of people's issues and start throwing in recipes that will work for your varied crowd.

While we started this chapter that talks about big projects and travel, think about how you can use this method to help you make better use of your time every day. I still maintain a Day-Timer, even as the entries are primarily personal. I plan menus with it, which allows me to make sure I've gone shopping for the ingredients or defrosted the necessary products. I make notes to remind me to get things done by a certain date; I schedule my annual physical and eye exams, etc. As a writer, I put down the chapter number on a date, which ensures I actually sit down and write it. I get the pleasure of crossing off my work as I get it done.

The two-page a day format is great, because on the right you have the hours of the day where you can slot appointments. On the left, you have more open space to list tasks. It can be helpful to slot the particularly unpleasant tasks into your calendar. E.g., "10:00-12:00 – start cleaning the house; 1:00-2:00 – rake the yard." When you do this, you tend to fill in the other spaces with fun stuff, such as "3:00-4:00 – get a discounted Frappucino at Starbucks during Happy Hour". I can look back at every day – even the ones where I sneaked in a nap – as being productive. I never have a day where I can't tell you what I did. I also know what's coming, so I can easily make plans. If your phone works for you, that's great. But if you aren't getting things done and feel frustrated, give paper a try.

Though it might seem like you'll need to invest in a big filing cabinet, much of the file contents can be recycled or shredded when the project is over. Everyone should have a shredder; we have to get rid of those pesky IRS files every year.

Give planning a try and see if you can't find a system that makes the time you spend more rewarding and memorable.

Unless commitment is made,
there are only promises and hopes;
but no plans.
—Peter F. Drucker, management consultant

Chapter 11

Maintaining Your Health

Time and health are two precious assets that we don't recognize and appreciate until they have been depleted.
—Denis Waitley, motivational speaker

Like many of you, I took my good health for granted when I was younger. I found every excuse to get out of P.E., even though without a car I had to walk to the mall, the library, and friends' houses. With a great home chef for a mother, I should have learned healthy eating habits, but stubbornness and picky tastes left me with a lot of bad ideas around food. Discovering Coke and French fries as a teen, my snacks made up for missed meals; I also discovered a variety of bad diets to keep my weight where I wanted it. Stillman's Quick Weight Loss, anyone? My friends and I shared many trips to Lake Anza and, more rarely, a friend's pool, where we slathered on cocoa butter to turn our skins brown and our hair golden.

With age came a bit of wisdom. I started going to Jazzercise in 1980 and found that, not only did the aerobic dance carve weight off me, but the after-work program made me a lot less hungry in the evening. I could eat what I wanted and still look good ... well, better ... than I had when I was younger. I had muscle definition. I have kept that up, but only late in the game adjusted my diet to reduce fat and increase fruits and vegetables. Why? After 40, losing weight is a constant struggle. Our metabolism slows and gravity takes a bigger toll. I also realized that, when I eat high quality ingredients, I'm able to eat less. One small truffle satisfies me instead of a large candy bar. Quality over quantity; that's my theory, and I'm sticking to it. Find a diet you can live with and which makes you feel good and then stick with it. However, remember that making a dramatic change in how you eat can take time.

I also began to learn a lot more about the supplements we all need, particularly as our appetites shrink and we get less and less of what we need from our food. Regular physical exams and unpleasant tests became a part of my world, all as I realized that enjoying my later years depended on more than the size of my 401-K.

Carissa had never dieted in her life, making her the envy of her friends. She ate what she wanted, whenever she wanted, exercised sporadically, and never saw a doctor except for the time she sprained her ankle. Her husband, Francisco, loved to joke about his "child bride." Aging also eluded her, until the day she tripped over a grandchild's toy and heard a snap.

"Francisco, help me," she screamed. The pain nearly made her lose consciousness. "This isn't a sprain," she said, thinking that she had fallen and couldn't get up years earlier than she had expected to make that statement.

At the Corpus Christi Urgent Care later that day, the doctor called her into his office. "You have a bad break, Carissa, one that requires surgery. But I'd like you to go for a bone density scan as soon as you can get there. The fall you took shouldn't have caused such a severe break."

Carissa didn't even have to hear the word osteoporosis to know what had happened. Invulnerable and eternal Carissa had finally discovering a weakness.

"I wonder what else they might find," Francisco said, after she had shared her news. "Maybe you need a complete physical.

At 53, Carissa could pass for her late 30's. But she began to suspect that her outer appearance belied her actual health.

"It's time to get serious. I need to find out what I can do to keep up with the family." She vowed to make a series of appointments as soon as she could get around.

We all find ourselves at the cusp of old age, beginning to pay the price for the choices we made throughout our lives. Studies say that the best chance we have for successful and prolonged aging starts in the womb, with the mother making all the right moves to give her baby the best chance. Each year we wait, we lose opportunities to armor ourselves against the bombardment of our environment against our bodies. Genetics and choices also play a role. But it's never too late to make a start. It's worth the effort, not only in terms of a longer life, but more importantly, a better quality of life. None of us really wants to spend the last 20 years of a long life in a nursing home ... nor can most of us afford to do so.

While it may look as if our fate is written in our genes, genetic predestination only goes so far. The environment plays a bigger role than we realized. The term to describe this impact is "epigenetics", which means the study of changes in organisms caused by modification of gene expression rather than alteration of the genetic code itself. While some environmental factors can alter the genes themselves, in most cases what changes is how they are expressed, or even if they are in fact expressed. Genes don't always determine destiny. An interesting example of this is the case of polydactyly, which shows up as extra fingers or toes. Although it is classed as an autosomal dominant gene, which means that if you have one copy from either parent you then have the condition, it isn't all that *expressive.* Most people with the gene never realize they have it, and most of those who see any result have only a stub of an extra digit. Read about an example of this with Henry VIII's second wife, Anne Boleyn.

Our choice of food and when we eat, how many hours of

sleep we get and how restful it is, how we choose to exercise, where and how we live, and aging itself can cause chemical changes which govern which genes turn on or off. In some cases, this is positive, as when healthy choices improve your ability to heal from injury. In others, such as many forms of cancer, the genes turned on or off take you from a healthy, normal state to a diseased state. What matters most is that, in most cases, epigenetics is reversible. We just don't know all the factors we need to address to heal ourselves of the worst issues, such as heart disease, cancer and Alzheimer's.

Still, even if we can't regain the rapid healing, resiliency and energy of our youth, we can often do a lot better than we are doing right now. The proof can be seen by looking at our grandparents and even our parents. For most of us, we remember them settling faster into old age than we are, giving up on the things they enjoyed earlier, and succumbing to minor illnesses when we find ourselves able to recover quickly. This can be attributed in part to our genes, but also to the better choices our parents made in raising us. Our parents knew a bit more about healthy eating and exercise than their own parents. We got vaccinated, so we didn't suffer the long-term impact of those childhood diseases. Many parents didn't smoke, or gave up smoking early on so that our lungs weren't impacted. And, while I've known a few people who worked in hard-core industries such as mining, which take years off their lives, we—and most of our parents—primarily suffered the stress of office politics, layoffs, and long commutes.

Studies have shown that the changes we can make have a "butterfly effect[1]," a model where small changes can yield noticeable improvements in our health. I noticed this when I began taking Jazzercise classes many years ago. My primary goal focused on weight loss without painful dieting. I knew that

---

[1] The Butterfly Effect: This effect grants the power to cause a hurricane in China to a butterfly flapping its wings in New Mexico.

it would take time. I never expected to sleep better and see faster healing and mood enhancement. Despite putting in a lot of work to get through the class—I didn't start in great shape—I felt increased energy even as I put out a lot. I found myself more resilient, happier, and more relaxed. All of these effects showed up in the first month of a regular program.

A recent study showed improvements in mortality in women who simply took regular walks. While my friends all know me as the pedometer junky who puts in at least 16,000 steps/day, and often 20,000+, the study proved that the benefit on mortality peaks out at a very achievable 7,500 steps/day[2]. It's important to note that this study didn't indicate the impact on weight loss; we usually need to work out more than that to achieve a good calorie burn. Check out what you do in a normal day, and then challenge yourself to take a walk every day. Start small, and then build on it. People who own dogs often enjoy longer, healthier lives simply because the dog must be walked. Sure, you can hit a dog park and just watch the dog run around. But you lose a lot when you just sit, even in nature.

One sign of aging is telomere shrinkage. Telomeres are the caps at the end of your chromosomes; as they shrink, we age. A German study proved that walking and other exercise can slow or reverse telomere loss[3]. But simple walking can do so much more. I've found that, when I feel stumped or just can't get going on something, a short walk will provide more rest and rejuvenation than a nap. Often, a problem I'm working on will be solved when I come home, even if I never consciously think about it. I get my best writing ideas on walks. Studies show that walking in nature can produce measurable increases

---

[2] https://jamanetwork.com/journals/jamainternalmedicine/article-abstract/2734709

[3] https://www.inverse.com/article/51255-anti-aging-workouts-telomeres

in joy – we can all use that!

If walking or organized exercise isn't your thing, don't worry. Dancing can be a powerful tool in anti-aging as well. Find something you enjoy doing that gets you moving and pushes you a little, and you will get what you need from that. Figure out the time of day when you feel most comfortable with a workout and put it on your calendar. Try yoga; none of us are as flexible as we were in our 20s. Yoga is a great workout with a powerful way to extend your active time by making your muscles and tendons stretch. Make time for exercise and you'll end up with more time in your day because your energy level will be so much higher. Remember that old saying, "feed a cold and starve a fever"? I believe in walking off a cold, but sleeping off a fever. Exercise engages your immune system to heal you faster. Exercise also armors your body so you don't get sick in the first place.

Next up is family and friendships. Studies prove that social interaction impacts both your health and your feeling of well-being.[4] Seek out positive interactions and get rid of relationships that suck the energy from you. Most of us have a few "remoras" in our acquaintance list, people who never initiate contact, cancel at the last minute, complain too much, or don't have time to listen when it's our turn to share a disappointment. Pull those suckers loose and free up your time to spend it with people whose friendship is beneficial.

One study, designed by Michigan State University psychology professor William J. Chopik, looked at two sets of data—one drawn from people around the world at different ages, and another from older Americans.[5] The first dataset came from

---

[4] https://www.nia.nih.gov/about/living-long-well-21st-century-strategic-directions-research-aging/research-suggests-positive

[5] https://www.sciencedaily.com/releases/2017/06/170606090936.htm

more than 270,000 volunteers, aged 15 to 99, from nearly a hundred countries. The volunteers answered questions about how highly they valued different kinds of relationships and how happy they were. Instead of tracking the same people over time, it tracked "representative" groups of different ages at intervals over the years.

The result: From about age 65 on, valuing friendship highly turned out to make a bigger difference than it did when you were younger. Strong family ties were linked to happiness, but their importance stayed about the same over the life span.

A challenge we've all faced as we got older is that it can be very hard to make new friends. In school days, constant contact with people and the requirement to interact made the job easy. While we may encounter a lot of people in our day, deepening the relationship beyond a curt greeting may prove more challenging. In some cases, simply finding new people to speak with can be hard. Remember that moving requires starting the process over.

Start the process by identifying what you hope to gain in a relationship. Are you looking for golf partners? Someone to travel with? Couples to share dinners, activities and vacations with? Understanding the need you bring will be important in designing your approach. Next, consider what you're prepared to offer. What makes you a great traveling companion? Can you cook a to-die-for meal? Are you a good shoulder to cry on, a fix-it god or a patient playing partner? When you know what you want and what you can offer, the way to approach people becomes clearer. In many cases, MeetUp groups can provide the contacts you need. (http://www.meetup.com) With a wide variety of interests, you're sure to find a group that matches your interests, thus meeting people in your area you might never have found on your own. Various online neighborhood groups also increase your reach, such as the popular NextDoor app.

Not into apps and online outreach? Then see what activities are offered in your community, especially your local library. If you find it hard to start conversations on your own, bring someone with you. Often that will break the ice. But reach out. Loneliness is frequently cited as a problem as we age, but it's one we should work on while we're still mobile and active.

Motivation may be an issue. As social as I am, I often feel like skipping an event or a party, hesitating even as I'm preparing to leave. I've never regretted pushing myself to go; I always have a great time. Even when things don't work out exactly as I'd hoped, there's always a funny story to tell about the scene. Make the effort. Look for things to do. Even your local street art fair might be a way to reach out. Taking a break from looking at art, you might grab a drink or a snack and end up chatting with someone nearby. These connections feed your spirit and your body.

As an extrovert, I feed on social interaction. However, for introverts "crowd" time requires energy. If this is you, you might get just as much benefit from interaction with a single person as with a group. Even at a party, find someone with common interests and share a quiet spot where you're not in the middle of things. After, take some time for yourself to recharge.

Part of managing your health as you age is making sure you give your body the fuel it needs to sustain and repair itself. Most of us just don't eat enough of what we need, and it gets worse as our appetites shrink with age and we have to cut back just to keep our weight in the healthy range. Often, our food doesn't provide what it used to in terms of nutrients, so we need to look at supplementation to help us age well.

I'll provide more details in Appendix C to help those who wish to learn more about supplements, but you'll find the high-lights here. To start, get a good multi-vitamin. Many brands now offer vitamins targeted to older adults; choose one of these. If you have trouble swallowing larger pills, look for the gummy version of any of the supplements; manufacturers know that people may struggle to swallow larger pills, particularly as we age, and where possible they do offer alternative ingestion methods. D-3 has been recently shown to make a huge difference in many aspects of your health, such as to ensure peak functioning of muscles, bones, digestion, immunity, hormones, and circulation. Probiotics can help a lot with digestion as well. Since your digestive system is your "second brain," feeding it well is essential.[6] A good gut efficiently absorbs what you need and disposes of what you don't.

Many good books have been written on this subject, but my final suggestion is to prioritize sleep. We all need different amounts, but most people really need about eight hours. That time should be continuous, uninterrupted and peaceful, so that your body and mind can use the interval to repair and restore. I remember people telling me that you sleep less when you age, which I took to mean you needed less. Nothing could be further from the truth. It's just a bit harder to get what you need. I sleep far more lightly, and noises will disturb my sleep. I've learned a few tips that might help you sleep better, too.

Drink a lot less as bedtime nears to help your bladder stay quiet.

Put devices away early and keep your phone on mute or away from your bedroom.

Consider investing in a pair of glasses that blocks blue light. Most prescription glasses can have this added, and non-prescription glasses are available.

Keep your room cool. We have a digital timer device that we plug into our fan, which allows us to set it for a certain number of hours or continuously. The device includes a remote. If the cold wakes me, I can quickly turn it off without

---

[6] https://www.hopkinsmedicine.org/health/wellness-and-prevention/the-brain-gut-connection

completely disturbing my sleep.

Move as many devices out of your bedroom as possible, including your television.

Watch the 6:00 news and skip the 11PM version. Stressful TV can make you anxious, even if you aren't conscious of it. A good comedy show is a better finale. I also like to read a chapter or two of a book; I always choose fiction, which makes me think a bit less.

Invest in a pillow that really supports your head, one you don't find yourself bunching up or redesigning to make you comfortable.

Go to bed and wake approximately the same time every day. When I first didn't need to wake up early I began to play with getting up later. Once I went back to a regular schedule, I felt better and slept better.

Take your health as seriously as you took saving for retirement. You'll be rewarded with more active years and more fun.

True silence is the rest of the mind, and is to the spirit what sleep is to the body, nourishment and refreshment.
—William Penn, writer

Chapter 12

Maintaining Your Brain

Out of all the things I have lost, I miss my mind the most.
—Mark Twain, writer

Perhaps the things we fear most is the loss of mental capacity as we age. In my 50s, I blamed "meno-brain" for frequent memory losses. My friends and I laughed about how we had lost our nouns and names. It seems less funny as I age. Once you've met someone with dementia or Alzheimer's, every misstep can scare you into believing you're at the first stages of the disorder. For many of us, we're concerned that losing mental capacity will be an inevitable part of aging. While our memories may not be as sharp, there's plenty we can do to keep our brains functioning. We can improve our odds with a few important steps.

Martin had reason for concern. His older sister, Jayda, died in her 50s of early-onset dementia. Almost overnight, this high-functioning software developer had to quit her job; she could no longer make sense of the work. The first sign came when she got lost on the way to work. Martin never forgot her call telling him that she had gotten lost and didn't know how to describe her location.

Doctors told him that, as he had made it to 65, this fast-moving disease was no longer an issue for him. But he realized that he wanted to try to ensure he didn't fall prey to any other brain problems. A single man, he had no one to call or to care for him if he began to fail.

"Time to make a plan," he said. Martin consulted his doctors and some reliable websites for suggestions on what he could do to improve his mental functioning. He learned that he was doing a lot of things right, but could do more. He swiftly added what he learned to improve his chances, such as finally investing in hearing aids and taking more walks in the Ann Arbor countryside.

Start with stimulating your mind. When we had regular jobs, we found it easy to keep learning and staying challenged. Without a manager assigning you tasks, you'll have to take over the job and find ways to keep your mind active. Read, but push yourself beyond "beach reading." Take classes either locally at the community centers in your area or online. Master Class (http://www.masterclass.com) can be a great choice. You'll learn from a wide variety of famous authors, chefs, actors, performers and more. A free or low-cost option is a MOOC—massively open online classes—which are available from universities. Mix it up, and try new hobbies as well. You should want to challenge your body as well as your mind, because even physical activities require mental effort. A perfect example is dancing, which engages your heart, your body and your brain. [1]

The more novel activities you engage in the more neural connections you make, and may also build a reserve of new neurons. This increases your "neural plasticity", which enables you to rebound even from cell loss. Do what you enjoy, but keep trying new things. Variety forces your brain to work harder.

As much as exercise helps to maintain your body, it's equally critical to your brain. Exercise can help you build new

---

[1] https://www.health.harvard.edu/mind-and-mood/12-ways-to-keep-your-brain-young

blood vessels to make sure your blood circulates well, even to your brain. Working out also builds new neurons and connections, just as mental exercises do. Lowering your blood pressure, blood sugar, weight, and even cholesterol, also positively impact your brain functioning. Get a baseline physical to know where you are with these key indicators of health.

While health clubs and classes can be great, spend some of the time outside, in nature. The benefits of being outside on stress, heart health and other factors will also affect your brain. No system operates alone. Want to shave years off your brain age? A study showed that six months of moderate exercise, such as walking, improved the following types of functions: ability to pay attention, regulate behavior, and be organized and get things done.[2]

Eating better will not only help you maintain the lower numbers you seek, such as blood pressure, A1C and weight, but it also reduces the risk of dementia. A Mediterranean diet can be particularly helpful. While you're at it, try to quit smoking. Watch your drinking. While a glass of wine with dinner can be healthy, boredom can lead to an increased desire to drink. Too much alcohol can undo all the good you've done in building new neurons and connections. You can preserve the myelin sheath of your neurons by drinking lots of water and reducing omega-6s (found in cooking oils, fatty red meat, processed foods). Drinking green tea, sleeping well and losing weight will help your memory as well.

Keep up with friends and family. Engaging in conversation and activities with others stimulates your brain as well. If you've withdrawn to some extent, get your hearing checked. Many people don't realize they have a hearing issue; they simply don't enjoy being around people. Not only will your active

---

[2] https://consumer.healthday.com/fitness-information-14/walking-health-news-288/just-6-months-of-walking-may-boost-aging-brains-740826.html

life improve with more engagement, but studies prove that, when you can't hear, you're more likely to develop dementia. Though the cause isn't clearly understood, the correlation is very high.

Socializing should be personal. Engage in person where possible; a phone call can be a reasonable substitute. Facebook friends won't satisfy the need for engagement. Use the Internet to start to reconnect with friends and family, but make a point of finding a way to meet with them. If you have to travel alone, select options that will let you travel with others. Road Scholar (formerly Elder Hostel) creates group itineraries offering support and community. Cruises can be a great way to connect.

Having a life purpose becomes even more essential as we age. Your purpose can be simple, such as to care for your grandkids or to grow a spectacular garden of food you can enjoy. Volunteering might serve that role. But define a purpose and actively advance it. At the same time, you want to "live in the moment," savoring what is in front of you at any given time. When your memories arise, connect with the great moments instead of the sad. Use all your senses, even as some of them may be sub-optimal. Really taste and enjoy your food. Take the time to enjoy nice aromas and comment on them.

Find a gerontologist to get an assessment on your brain health. As we age, we all lose a lot of short-term memory capability, which can be scary. It's easy to think it's something more serious than it is. There's a big difference between normal memory issues and Alzheimer's. If you are concerned, find someone who has been highly recommended and get yourself checked out. Even consider a second opinion. For myself, I started having memory issues in my 50s as I went through menopause. I've never been great at remembering names; then it seemed to be a lot worse, and I also found I struggled sometimes with nouns. With no other issues, I discovered that

I suffered from normal aging. Some people do better than others; don't compare yourself to others.

As in the prior chapter, supplements can help. For men, get your testosterone checked: low T values can lead to brain cell death and increase the amyloid-B proteins found in Alzheimer's. Low estrogen in women has been shown to lead to memory issues, but no permanent problems. If your thyroid isn't producing as well as previously, you can experience memory loss, fatigue, increased cold sensitivity, apathy and weight gain. Vitamin D-3 makes a big difference in keeping dementia at bay. Magnesium energizes the brain, while B-complex is essential to healthy neurons and nerves, Omega-3 (fish oil) makes cell membranes healthier. Multi-strain probiotics, especially those containing Bifidobacterium, lactobacillus and mycobacterium vaccae, protect your brain from the negative effects of stress.

A recent study has shown that lithium orotate in small doses can protect against dementia. Consult with your doctor before starting a lithium regime to ensure it doesn't conflict with any of your existing medicines and to get a proper dosage recommendation.

As we lose some capabilities, you can use a trick or two to help you out. Post-it notes are one of life's greatest inventions. Invest in them and post reminders to yourself on the calendar of your choice. Write down appointments, tasks and events. Use the smart capabilities of the Internet to help you, such as sites such as Birthday Alarm, which will send you an email to remind you of important appointments. Expect that you won't remember everything, and then plan accordingly.

Everything we do for our health is interconnected and. with care, we can enjoy many good years. Keep your brain healthy, while also taking steps to help your memory along. It's not easy, and it's frequently frustrating, but you can do more than you think you can to keep your brain cells thriving.

Chapter 13

Reclaiming Your Creativity

Creativity is intelligence having fun.
—Albert Einstein, scientist

Think you're not creative? Perhaps the problem is that you're defining creativity too narrowly. The word only means using your imagination to make something new. While people often limit it to "the arts" and artists, every one of us is inherently creative. Look at children. They constantly invent new things and play with new ways of thinking about things. "Play" is the operative word. Creativity makes life much more interesting and rewarding. When you are thinking creatively, you expand your perceptions and can more easily face challenges. And it's just fun.

Many studies have shown that we are born creative, but school, rules, and external judgment try to defeat the urge except in the most determined and persistent. Yet, it can't be eliminated from our brains, only deterred somewhat. Ever find a clever solution to a perplexing problem? You had to be creative to do that. As we age, many of us find that we no longer care as much what other people think of us, which is the first step in embracing your creative self.

Victor never thought of himself as creative. In 40 years as an accountant in Denver, he'd never felt the urge to draw or write a novel. His wife, Tess, always called him the brains of the operation. Tess could sketch little cartoons that always amused their kids and illustrated letters and cards. Their home computer terrified her, and Victor had to be the fix-it guy around the house. He did numbers and she did art. It worked well ... until Victor retired.

Knowing that he should have a hobby, he took a variety of classes, trying to learn how to draw and then how to make pottery. Nothing resonated, and he happily dumped his creations as soon as the classes ended.

"Hey, not everyone has to be creative, do they?" he asked his friend, Tom, at a tailgate party.

"But you are," Tom said.

"Right. The creative accountant. Not a label I want."

"But that's exactly it. You have been so creative, while keeping it legal. All your clients pay fewer taxes because you always think outside the box."

Victor considered his words. Maybe creativity didn't just mean creating art. He decided to look at any activities that made him think, that made him come up with new ideas.

You're creative when you have to come up with a new way of looking at something or doing something. Engineers create constantly, seeing a better way to accomplish a task, a more elegant approach. Home cooks constantly create, as they figure out substitutions for missing ingredients or how to turn a refrigerator full of odds and ends into a delicious meal. It all counts. The challenge is identifying where you can enjoy being creative and do more of it. Start by getting out of your rut. What's another way to do one of a hundred things you have to do every day? For example, a different way to walk or drive. I've enjoyed taking a street-side walk, choosing my next steps at each corner by which way the lights are green. By not making decisions, I've found this to be a moving meditation. This method triggers something in me that causes new ideas to pop.

I've always written, so it really didn't seem like I was creative. It was just me. However, I can't draw anything, and actually failed at art in grammar school. I was middle of the class in singing and playing piano, and only cast in parts in school plays because they pretty much cast everyone. I found myself admiring people I thought of as artists, without noticing that people really liked the photographs I took. I have an eye for it, when I work at it. I'm also a huge fan of the TV show "Chopped," taking every challenge as a chance to see what I might make with the odd ingredients. It makes me more creative in designing menus, reconfiguring recipes, and making things out of my head. You can't write all day long; there's time to do more.

Why be creative? Creativity is a great way to make the brain work and keep functioning optimally. But it's also fun and fairly addictive. Once you begin to imagine, it's hard to stop. And once in a while, more often with practice, you can find yourself in "flow," a mental state where you are so fully immersed in an activity, so absorbed and in love with what you are doing, that you lose track of time. Mihály Csíkszentmihályi coined the term, but of course, people have been in flow throughout history. The best discoveries have been made when inventors experienced flow. But it's open to everyone.

Lost in my writing, I can work for hours, only coming out of it when I realize I'm: a. hungry; b. thirsty; or c. hurting because I tend to hunch over the PC. And yet, the buzz continues and inspires me to greater success in everything I do the rest of the day. It works when you bring an open, innovative mind to a task, whatever the task might be.

We're forced to be creative in most jobs. Small budgets, too few people, and limited time for a project make us experts at it. Don't leave your creativity behind in your job. Bring it with you into retirement and experience more joy, every day.

You can't use up creativity. The more you use the more you have.
—Maya Angelou, poet and activist

Chapter 14

Discover and Add New Strengths

With the new day comes new strength and new thoughts.
—Eleanor Roosevelt, diplomat and activist

One thing we can count on throughout our lives is that many of our interests will change. Untapped strengths may have a chance to grow as we try out new interests and activities. During our work lives, free time was precious. Now, it's all free time, so try anything that remotely interests you. You just never know what hidden talents you might find. Claude Monet produced his best work in his 70s, as did Grandma Moses. Harlan David Sanders founded Kentucky Fried Chicken at age 65, Clara Peller gained advertising fame at age 81 in the Wendy's TV commercial, "Where's the beef?"
https://www.youtube.com/watch?v=riH5EsGcmTw
There are countless stories of many who found their sweet spot only after their careers stopped interfering with their lives.

Chao grew up with strict dictates. He could become a doctor or an engineer. Moving with his family to Silicon Valley in his teen years, he found it easy to translate his engineering skills to IT, moving easily from hardware design to architecture and finally to mobile design. While he enjoyed it and certainly loved the pay, something was missing.

In his late 50s, he and his wife, Sun, began to enjoy the fun of being childfree. They'd long discussed all the things they could do and where they could live. Austin sounded great; he could transfer to a great job there AND eliminate some of his awful commute. Then, Sun had a stroke. Her slow recovery forced Chao to take over the many house responsibilities while juggling his job. While he hated house-cleaning with a passion, he found that preparing the evening meal presented a new challenge for him, one he enjoyed. Cooking had never been something he knew how to do, but he took to it readily.

"All those cooking shows you made me watch paid off," he told Sun, tenderly feeding her his latest creation.

"You're a natural. If I had only known how well you could cook," she said.

Chao thought about it over the next years. Even after Sun made a good recovery, he continued to prepare dinner, daring himself to make more complex meals and try new ingredients and cuisines. As he retired, he wondered whether he couldn't do something with his cooking prowess. Having spent time with the chefs at his last job at Google, he decided to see if he could apprentice with one of them. In a short time, he fell into the kitchen groove. To celebrate, Sun gifted him with training at the Culinary Institute. Chao had found the creative spark of cooking rejuvenated him.

Your long-undiscovered abilities might not lead to a new job, but could inspire a new passion. Taking classes at adult education centers is a great way to figure out what you'd like to try next. Non-writers have found a hidden talent when they tried a memoir writing class. Many non-athletes have been shocked to discover how well-designed their bodies are to endurance events, which take a different talent than sprints. Some of the first-time triathlon or distance runners only started training in their 40s, and there are events for older people. You'll hear of amazing feats by men and women in their 70s and 80s, most of whom never considered themselves capable of athletic skill.

Some people wait until they actually retire, but part of retirement planning should be figuring out what you want to do next *before* you stop working. That means reassessing your strengths. Although I had a long, successful career in IT, I never felt it drew on my best abilities. I knew I could write and, fortunately, that's something you can do while you work. Isn't that what those long, boring staff meetings were created for? But I realized that, as much as I liked to write, I liked to talk with people and, if possible, offer them help. I started with a plan to become a therapist, but ended up opting to become a life coach instead. Taking night classes after a full day of work might not have been the easiest thing I could have chosen. In my 50s, I found it harder to concentrate at night, the only time I had to do homework. But I had an inspirational model. My mother got her law degree in her 50s, a much higher bar than the one I aimed for.

But finding new strengths isn't just about all-encompassing passions. By testing your interests to broaden the scope of what you can spend your time doing, you'll find abilities and interests you never expected. It might mean taking some classes, and, if you're really dedicated, it might lead to another career. But it doesn't have to. Test yourself. On your next walk, slow it down and spend more time looking at nature. Does anything grab you? Bring some binoculars and see if you don't find a fascination with birds. If cooking meals has become a chore, have some fun on the Net and type in a bunch of ingredients that got lost in your fridge. Add the word "recipe" and search. Buy a new cookbook, picking a cuisine you know little about. My cooking became more inspired the tougher the challenge I gave myself. Now, we regularly have fun with molecular gastronomy, *sous vide*, and other interesting cooking options.

We don't have just one talent. If you'd asked me, I'd say I'm a good writer, but I'm so much more. And so are you. Do things you've never done just to see if you'll like them. Try SNUBA on your next beach vacation; it's a great test to see if you'd like scuba. Find a friend who plays a sport you've never tried. You might have a natural talent for golf. Try out for a part in a play or join a singing group. MeetUp is another great vehicle to find interesting new ways to spend time. You'll never know unless you try. In the course of your attempts, you'll find those new strengths as well as new interests. There's just so much untapped talent in each of us, and now we have the chance to figure it out.

Adversity also reveals our strengths, but life will simply throw that out at us. We don't have to seek it out. And yet, those strengths can deepen relationships and give you new perspective. I never used to know what to say to people who were grieving after a loss. I cared, but I didn't have the words. It made me feel useless and less of a good friend. When my mother died, my experience with that transformed my feelings about grieving, and I now find that the words I need are there. I know what to say to each person, from my heart, and with empathy and compassion. I've also found that, while each new loss in our lives hits us hard, the first bad one gives us a chance to recognize and hone our strengths so that we can mine our own deep resources.

As a result of too-busy, demanding lives, one strength that many of us have never developed is the ability to enjoy and get benefit from leisure. Ever feel guilty for letting hours just drift away? I know that's one of my issues. With time, you can learn to relish the chance to read a book in peace, take a nap in a hammock, mix an adult beverage mid-afternoon and sit in the garden sipping it till all the ice melts. Enjoyment is a strength, a muscle that we all need to firm up.

Chapter 15

To Move or Not

*If we were meant to stay in one place,
we'd have roots instead of feet...*
—Rachel Wolchin, blogger and writer

As we get older, our housing needs and interests change. You may have picked a location because it was near your office or in a great school district. Some choices are driven by affordability. While you had children, you needed a bigger place. While not everyone moves in retirement, it's definitely a question you want to contemplate. Downsizing may be a great option, potentially freeing up money. Some move to be closer to family; others move to get farther away. And if the reason you live where you do now no longer applies, this might be the time to ask the question: "Where to next?"

Rex and Jeanine had always loved traveling to Hawaii. Nearly every year, they spent a few weeks on one of the islands. They planned a trip to find a place they would love on Oahu, as it had the most support services. Jeanine insisted they live in a place with good medical care, a decision Rex understood. Lucking into a distress sale and enjoying the break from the high property taxes they struggled with in New Jersey, they signed a purchase agreement. Time to move.

At first, Hawaii felt like a dream to them. Getting up to snorkel nearly every day, playing golf and sitting on their deck with a drink at night; what could be better? The prices at the stores surprised them, even for items that purportedly came from Hawaii, such as fish and pineapple. Traffic reminded them of the New Jersey Turnpike and kept them away from Honolulu most of the time. Jeanine began to reach out to neighbors, hoping to enjoy the friendly relationships she had developed back home, but few people reciprocated. Making friends had never been an issue before, but in this new place, they both struggled.

Uday and Amara decided to downsize, first looking for a smaller place in a quieter suburb in Connecticut where they had lived for many years. They loved the proximity to New York City and planned to enjoy going there more often to take advantage of cultural activities and fine dining. They thought they would be able to net a good amount of money from their house, but as they began to look, the places they liked cost more than they wanted to spend and the high property taxes discouraged them. Driving farther out, they discovered a charming community in Rhode Island. The property taxes were only slightly lower, but they could buy the place they wanted for a lot less.

They assessed the place, renting a cottage through AirBnB for a while to figure out if they really liked the people and the community. Once they realized it would work for them, they put their house on the market and moved. Still a short commute to New York, Amara knew they had found a home. Their kids loved that Mom and Dad still lived close enough to visit.

To move or not may be the biggest decision you have to make at this point in your life. The best approach is to start by listing why you might want to move. What do you hope to gain from a new location or type of housing situation? What factors matter most to each of you? What might be a deal killer? What's in it for you to stay just where you are? The options can feel daunting; you have so many things to consider.

In deciding to stay, you want to consider the affordability

of your place as well as the desirability. Have you paid off the mortgage? Can you afford the taxes and other costs of the house? Will you be able to keep up with the maintenance and cleaning as you age? Do you have strong ties to the community? Does the place you live support older people by providing amenities such as senior dial-a-ride, good health care and senior activities? Is your place two-story? By clearly defining why you like where you are and how the location fits your new lifestyle, you can firm up the decision to stay. But by assessing the situation, you may find that staying won't serve you. Too many people stay because their children or friends live nearby, only to see them eventually move away. That factor alone can't be the reason to stay.

I'm in the process of considering a move. I never upsized, so downsizing wouldn't be an issue. For me, the value of a move would be to get into a place that better supports my needs and desires as I age. I'm looking at 55+ communities and CCRCs (continuing care retirement communities) as the best options for me and my husband. One of my core needs is friendship, and it's far easier to make friends in a place designed for that purpose. Both types of communities offer many activities as well as allowing residents to define new ones and attract neighbors to join them. I'd like to find a lower cost, lower tax state to make more out of my retirement funds. For many years, I lived in California because I worked here; it always felt easier to stay than go. But other communities align better with my values, and what work I do now could be done anywhere. Thank you, Worldwide Web.

Part of my plan will be to visit each of the places I might consider and spend some time assessing them for what I need. I will check out hospitals, parks and hiking trails, grocery stores, and the proximity of a good airport. I'll try to chat up people to see if I get a good sense of community. But my plan starts with a list. What do I need to be happy somewhere else?

We forget so often what we take for granted where we live, but we need to delineate those items so we can make a good decision.

For years, I talked about how great it would be to live in Sedona, AZ. It's one of the few places I've traveled to over and over again. In reality, it fails on so many of my criteria while still being one of the most beautiful places I've ever been. Hospitals are distant, Flagstaff doesn't have that great of an airport, and Phoenix is three hours away. And the desirability of the place has led to major traffic snarls as more people discover it. Housing in Sedona is expensive. While we'll probably visit again, Sedona is not on my list of retirement destinations.

When we travel, we can fall in love with places. But vacations aren't real life. Many retirement communities offer a chance to stay in one of their properties for a few days or more. That's a great way to evaluate the property and also the surrounding area. Test it against the list you made so you can evaluate how good a match the location will be. As many retirement communities offer the same amenities, the negatives may end up driving your decision.

What weather can you live with? Do you like seasons? What hobbies will you enjoy in the future, and can you do them where you move? Begin this journey by asking yourself a lot of questions, and consider what you enjoy doing and need day-to-day where you are now. You'll have to find new doctors, hairdressers, stores, public transit options, etc. Take time to make your list of desires, must-haves, and deal-killers before every starting to look. Then you'll have the criteria to test every option.

Baby Boomers have reinvented retirement housing options as well, so you have more to choose from. Some people feel happiest in a regular community with a mix of ages. New options exist where created communities with varied age groups have their own space, but shared areas to enjoy. A great term for this is "intergenerational ingenuity solutions." More options are built every day where you can share in the lives of people of all ages.

Builders keep developing new 55+ communities, so there's probably one wherever you might want to live. People choose these to develop new friendships, enjoy planned activities, and have a little more support. The CCRCs are a newer development and have many pluses, but also a few issues you need to consider. As Baby Boomers age, the demand for assisting living and memory care keep increasing, and many of us struggle with finding a place willing to take an aging parent. Affordability can be a major issue. Elder care isn't cheap. A CCRC offers you a guarantee of continuing care. You begin as an independent resident, and then, when you need it, you can move to an assisted living or memory care center right on the property. Monthly fees are assessed to cover the maintenance of the property, home care, quite often a meal a day in onsite restaurants, and other amenities. You'll pay these fees forever. And the upfront buy-in doesn't give you ownership. In most cases, you have purchased only a life-interest in your place. If you wanted to leave a large inheritance to your children, this choice will reduce your estate value. However, it does mean that you will never be a burden on your children, nor require them to figure out how to take care of you if aging presents mental or physical challenges. My father made this choice, and it was the best gift he could have given my sister and me. These places can be much nicer than the standalone facilities. One potential hurdle: CCRCs demand a health check before they accept you. If this option looks good to you, make sure to move before you start having health issues. Because of the guarantee they offer, they expect you to come in with your faculties fully in order.

In these examples, I'm talking about buying a new place,

but you also have the option to rent. An important consideration to keep in mind is rising costs. Once you buy a place (or buy into a CCRC), you've got that expense under control. And, if you own it, you can apply for a reverse mortgage, if it makes sense, to further fund your retirement. But renting may be an option for some people.

When you move, you have several options to consider for your old property. Many people sell, but depending on where you live, capital gains can be an issue. Renting your former home can work if you aren't moving far away and want to manage it, or are willing to invest in a property manager. Having an additional source of income can be a great decision for many people, and will be particularly lucrative if you live in an area where housing is at a premium. A final option is to put your money in a charitable trust. The trust will buy you an annuity which will pay you a fixed amount for the rest of your life. The tax benefits of this option could be attractive to some.

As you consider a move, keep in mind the all-in cost of moving. In most cases, you'll have to fix up your place, unless you are donating it. At this point, we can't ask our friends to gather and pack us up and help us move. We need to hire help. It's a great time to start downsizing your "stuff." I stopped gift exchanges with friends years ago (we give each other events and get-togethers instead) because I realized I already had more stuff than I needed. I regularly go around and find things to donate. It's easier if you already have less and there are tons of people who need and want your furniture, books, clothes, etc.

Another factor, both for downsizers and those who simply want to reduce the cost of moving, is getting rid of your excess clothing, furniture, books, hobby projects, etc. It can be very tough to do this quickly; we all have loads of accumulated memories and joy tied up in our things.

A useful tool may be the Spark Joy methodology of Marie

Kondo. https://konmari.com/ She has developed a methodology for cleaning, organizing and discarding that many find helpful. Plan ahead; begin today.

Moving may be the biggest decision you need to make at this point in your life, but don't delay it. Not only do you have more options when you are a bit younger, you also have the ability to move. Too many people age in place, watching a formerly lovely neighborhood degenerate into chaos. As it becomes time to give up driving, people find they don't have great options to get around.

The good news is that you have so many choices. The bad news is … you have too many choices. Make the choice early and take the time to do it right. It's probably not something you ever want to do again.

Chapter 16

Ways to Stay Connected

Friendship is born at that moment when one person says to another, 'What! You too? I thought I was the only one.'
—C.S. Lewis, writer and theologian

Anyone else notice how hard it is to make new friends? When we were in school, friendship seemed effortless. Part of what made it easy was being constantly around the same people. Instead of having to "cold call" a stranger, you sat near them, partnered with them on projects, perhaps formed study groups. Getting to know someone stretched gradually over a long semester, culminating in friendship, if you had enough in common. At work, some of the same rules applied, though you might have encountered people who didn't care to make friends through work. Others made friends because their kids were friends.

Suddenly, you're on your own. Many of us live in places where neighbors are strangers and you can pass an entire day without interacting with anyone beyond what's needed to get things done. As I've noted, this isn't enough for your mental or physical health. And yet, it's hard to make the kinds of connections that will deepen into friendships.

Kurt's wife had died in a traffic accident when she was only 48. Hating the idea of dating, he busied himself with work and delayed retirement as long as possible. At work, he had colleagues to go to lunch with. A few old friends invited him to dinner or to a kid's sporting event once in a while, but one by one, most of them moved away, some to be closer to grand-kids, others no longer interested in staying in Pennsylvania.

Kurt's two children had never really forgiven him for the accident. It hadn't been his fault. Still, he had insisted they go out late one night to pick up something at the store, something either could have picked up alone. He just wanted the company. A drunk driver broadsided the passenger door just a few blocks from their home. In any event, his kids lived across the country from him and he didn't really enjoy flying.

A few weeks into retirement, Kurt recognized that he had been sleeping in and napping every afternoon. He realized he just didn't have anything he wanted to do if he had to be alone. That afternoon, he ran into an old work colleague at the grocery store.

"How're you doing, Kurt?" Mitch asked.

"Okay, I guess. Can you get that I'm actually missing work sometimes."

"Tell me about it. My wife has a honey-do list a mile long. The worst project we've done looks more attractive than all the crap she wants me to do."

Kurt smiled. "Got time for a cup of coffee? You could always say you couldn't find everything on her list and had to go to another store."

They sat sipping a cup of coffee and talking about retirement. Mitch mentioned that he had begun to look up old friends on Facebook.

"Hate the application, but it can be useful. I'm finding others who want to get out of the house."

They made plans to play a round of golf the next weekend, and Kurt promised he'd start looking at Facebook as well.

Facebook, LinkedIn, and other social media sites may be a place to start. If you're bored or lonely, perhaps others you know or were friendly with in the past might be too. And if not, they might include you in activities they have planned. It helps if you know things you want to do, ideas that you haven't explored because they're more fun with someone else. This kind of problem can be a bigger issue if you retire early and all your friends still work. But still, they might like to get together on the weekends or even occasionally on a week night. But you have to reach out.

Staying connected with friends takes some time and effort. People can be very forgiving even if you haven't reached out in a while, but be prepared to be curious about them first. In any given situation, leading with your "ask" brings less optimal results than by leading with your curiosity. Find out what they're up to and what they plan to do next. Target a short meet—coffee, a movie, lunch. Rebuild the relationship one step at a time. And come prepared with your ideas.

One way to keep connected is something most of us have sadly abandoned—the Christmas letter. While we might have laughed at the early bragfests, in most cases it was interesting to keep up with people in this way. The letter represented a handshake, reaching out once a year to people you cared about. Even a short message keeps a relationship alive. It's never too late to start this. Emails can also be great conversation starters, if you have their email addresses. This is where social media can come in handy. Your old LinkedIn network provides a way to reach out, and even retired people often list their email address on their site. It's easy to forget how many people you have known and cared about over the years, but when you make contact, you may be surprised to learn that they relish the exchange too.

When an old friend comes to mind, I immediately try to find them online. Surprisingly, many of them are going through a tough time when I contact them. It's like quantum mechanics' "spooky action at a distance." I think of them because their challenges perturb the tendrils that connect us to each other.

Often, the friend really needs support at that moment, and, as our mothers told us, "a friend in need is a friend indeed." This outreach can be the beginning of a new relationship. And even when the exchange is brief, having an opportunity think outside ourselves, to help someone else, can be healing and rewarding.

But what if you need friends where you live now but you don't know very many people? As mentioned in previous chapters, volunteering and signing up for MeetUps you might enjoy can be a fast way to meet a variety of people. Other options might be the local VFW or SIRS chapter for men. For me, I've met a lot of my newest friends at Jazzercise. I confess this never happened at a health club, but in the local classes like Jazzercise and Zumba, women enjoy hanging out there and chatting with each other. It's our "Cheers" bar, where everyone knows your name.

Take every opportunity to talk with people and reach out when someone needs a hand. I grew up in the Midwest, where we all knew our neighbors and everyone ran out to help when someone's car got frozen in the driveway or a newcomer started to bring hot water out to an ice-laden tree. When you reach out, even in small ways, the beginnings of a friendship can develop. I regularly chat with people on transit, on the street, or in line at the grocery store. Just a friendly moment might turn into more. Places where you like to go may be places other people go to regularly as well.

If you love theater, local theaters often have special meet-and-greets on opening night. After the production, everyone shares the experience and it's another way to connect. I've met tons of people at the wine tasting events at Total Wine. Go to a cooking class; you can't possibly get through it without loads of conversation. Go where you want to be. Many people who love golf find that, when they are willing to play with someone else, they find a golf buddy for life.

Another old-school option may be letter writing. The Letter Exchange lets you pick from various ads and start a letter friendship. It's not uncommon to find that one of your pen pals lives nearby. And even if they don't, the exchange can be very rewarding. Often, letters move to email as you get to know each other better. You'll definitely enjoy the trip to the mailbox more when you might get a real letter from someone.

As you develop or redevelop your people-meeting skills, you'll be better prepared for the reality that people you care about sometimes move. And as we age, some of our friends will die. But when you know how to connect, you'll have a way to keep your circle of friends robust.

For those who move away, you may be starting over. If you choose your location carefully, assessing the friendliness and responsiveness of people in that area, you'll do better. And this is why the 55+ communities were invented. With all the activities, if you want friends, you'll make them. One friend told me that the day they moved into their new home, people came up to them and asked them if they didn't want to just throw their stack of boxes in their house and come over for some wine. It's been like that for them ever since. They only have free time when they say 'no' to something.

Another friend visited several possible locations before selecting a new home. As all the communities were gorgeous, the main factor influencing their choice was the friendliness of the people. When they got there, they found complete strangers offering to help them get new furniture delivered to their home, volunteering their own trucks.

We'll live longer and happier lives with people we care about around us. Make the effort to develop a few, good friendships. You'll never regret reaching out.

Chapter 17

Syncing with Your Partner

A worthy relationship is an agreement that
challenges and supports both participants.
—Joseph Rain, writer

All the assessments we've made thus far tap into what you
need to make your retirement great. As many people have
partners to consider, we need to talk about how to develop a
shared plan. Over time, we make assumptions about those we
love. At this turning point, those assumptions may prove to be
wrong. If you're traveling the retirement path alone, feel free
to skip this chapter.

Mei and Reo shared the joys of city life, appreciating the
close proximity of activities and restaurants. With jobs that de-
manded long hours, time mattered more than anything. They
tolerated the small apartment they could afford in Manhattan
as a better option than a long commute. Still, both regularly
complained about the lack of a study; they shared a space in
the small dining room.

When they felt they could afford to retire, Mei knew they
would relocate to the country where they could enjoy a larger
property with land for flowers as well as vegetables. She longed
to get her hands dirty again, as she had as a small child in
Hikone on the small plot of land they enjoyed. She'd already
located some nice places in Vermont and New Hampshire.

As they finalized dates with their respective companies, Mei
suggested they meet with her real estate agent to look at a

place to move. Reo's jaw dropped.

"Move? Who said anything about moving?"

"But we only live here for our jobs, right?" Mei said.

"We have everything we need here. The only thing we didn't have was an office each. Now we don't really need it," Reo said, his cheeks flushing with annoyance.

"You like living in New York?" she said.

"Where else can we have so much right at hand? As we get older, you'll love that you're only a short cab ride from everything. We don't have to worry about owning a car. Neither of us drives anyway."

Mei knew his arguments made sense, but she wanted to get away from the "City that Never Sleeps." Over the years, while Reo seemed never to hear it, she remembered few nights where the blaring of car horns and the police and ambulance sirens didn't wake her. She wanted more room for her hobbies and a place to grow something more than the sad cactus on their window sill.

Just as many engaged couples never talk about the most important things—babies, money, life dreams—many couples find they haven't discussed what retirement means to them until the day comes when work stops. While it rarely leads to divorce, compromises are just a part of the deal. The earlier you share your dreams, your ideas and your plans, the better. What you don't know will present numerous problems.

Successful couples such as Mei and Reo could have planned this long ago, starting to save for a small place to escape to, one that provided Mei with the outdoors and space she wanted. Mei actually loved city life; just not all the time. Many people compromise with two lifestyles, ones they can both sign up for. Another way to expand your options is with an RV or mobile home, traveling the country and experiencing a variety of locations, climates and activities. AirBnBs and VRBO can give you the feeling of being at home in places around the world.

As we age, we may find a lot of our beliefs and values start to change, a little or a lot. But what you don't share separates a couple. The people who keep talking are more likely to stay aligned than those who hold back their views. While it's better to be talking throughout your shared lives, not everyone does this.

If you are beginning to wonder about how well you and your partner are syncing up, know that conversation is critical at this point, along with careful listening. Go deep in these talks, understanding not just what your partner wants but what it means to them. The "why" can sometimes bridge into a different "how." A simple example of a resolved issue can help. One friend said her husband had an obsession with the toothpaste tube. It had to be squeezed from the bottom, then carefully rolled to get every drip of value from it. In the morning, with so much to do, she couldn't be bothered. They bought two tubes so each person could do it their own way. When she wanted to toss hers, he would take it and squeeze more out of it for himself. Look for the third way.

As you discuss your retirement dreams, keep focused on the passions you share. Also, prioritize your goals. Just as we do in everyday situations, if something isn't a high priority for you, consider letting your partner win. How much time do you really want to spend together? Is there room for doing things with friends or alone? You might be surprised as to how this unfolds. My husband and I traveled a lot during our work lives. He ended up being gone for a year at a time on three different occasions. I'm pretty independent; while I might have liked to have him around, I found my own way during these tough times. Guess I might have made a good military wife, too.

When we started moving towards retirement, I realized we were together almost all the time. Before we got to this point,

I had some concerns. Friends of mine who both worked and went to school at night seemed the happiest of couples. One day, school ended and they had more time together; soon, it became obvious, too much time. They agreed to an amicable divorce. I didn't expect to want someone around all the time, and I doubted anyone could stand large doses of me. To my surprise, both assumptions were wrong. Honesty and openness had always been core values in our relationship, and this meant we kept talking and checking in when we had more time together.

Expect to have many conversations about a variety of issues. Remember when you bought your first house together? I'm sure you didn't have the exact same agenda. How did you resolve things then? We're smarter now; we can do even better than in our early days so that, in the end, both of you feel like you have what you need. Be prepared to speak up. No matter how long you've lived together, neither of you is a mind reader. Make it clear to your spouse what you really want, and remember to ask what they want. When we try to please by anticipating or guessing someone else's desire, we're too frequently wrong.

Stay open to new ideas. Along the years, some of the best experiences my husband and I enjoyed came about when we allowed the other to share a passion with us. I'm not sure I'd be a scuba diver without Mike. I loved the idea, but without a guaranteed partner, couldn't see investing the time or the money. We've had some amazing dive trips ever since, including a magical time in the Red Sea. He's become a gourmet cook and an expert sous chef, enabling me to make more and more complex recipes because I can rely on a good set of extra hands. Our food experiences have helped us grow together. He's introduced me to shooting and to flying. I'm the health junky, keeping him exercising and—mostly—eating well. I'm guessing there are a few more adventures we'll share as I begin to have more free time to join him.

Testing out the "new" helps challenge both people; stepping out of your comfort zone will keep you young. Take classes together, or try a new sport together. Go someplace neither of you thought to try. Eat new cuisines; listen to music that isn't your usual. Explore. Grow. Learn.

COURSE
CORRECTIONS

Chapter 18

Becoming a Caregiver

*My caregiver mantra is to remember: the only control
you have is over the changes you choose to make.*
—Nancy L. Kriseman, geriatric social worker

You've made your retirement plans, perhaps deciding to move
or travel for an extended period. An aging parent calls and lets
you know that they need help. Or your partner develops a
medical issue that will inevitably alter your dreams. All at once,
your plans go on hold.

Esperanza's mother, Mila, had been the sturdy trunk of her
family, supporting all the branches so they could grow freely.
No one realized that her husband, Jose, had been the roots
holding the mighty trunk upright. When he died, Mila couldn't
function on her own. Miguel and Esperanza took her into their
home in Santa Fe, converting the guest room to a suite for her.
They regretted having downsized so quickly; the house felt
cramped with three people sharing the smaller space.

In charge her whole life, Mila couldn't adapt to the couple's
lifestyle and began imposing her will. Dinner would be at 5PM,
never later. It must include substantial portions of meat, vegetables, and home-made tortillas. She also expected desserts
frequently and a special dinner on Sunday. All her needs were
deemed "urgent" by her and, as she had given up her driver's
license, the two had to adjust their schedule to meet her needs.
Travel plans had to be abandoned, and even the daily activities
they had enjoyed had to be curtailed to meet her needs. The

situation didn't work for anyone.

Initially resistant to the idea, Mila began to warm to the idea of moving to assisted living after she visited a few properties nearby. Jose noted how lucky they had been to move to a much less expensive area. With a bit of help from the two of them, Mia could manage to live at a place of her choice, funding most of it with her small retirement savings. Initially, they found themselves spending time nearly every day visiting her, but slowly weaned her from this schedule as she became a part of her new community and started enjoying the daily activities provided.

Neil and Julie expected they would have to help one of their parents as they aged so they moved to Florida to be near them. Unfortunately, Julie had a severe stroke a year after retiring. Her recovery took a year and, even after all options had been exhausted, she still found she didn't have the energy or strength to return to her normal activities. Their plans to RV to golf courses in every state had to be abandoned.

Neil felt like he had worked harder that year than he ever had in his accounting practice. Even tax season took less of a toll than looking after his wife. He knew the year had been worse for Julie. She tried so hard not to make demands, but Neil knew he had never been good at caregiving. His solution had been to invest some money in having a care worker come over several times a week so he could get away, not just to shop, but also just to breath. After talking to others in a similar situation, he learned that burnout can be a serious issue. He decided that the money spent was an investment in their relationship.

When faced with becoming a caregiver, very few people look forward to the challenge. Most of us have no training, and for many, such as myself, we know that patience isn't our strong suit. When you love someone, you have to do the right thing. However, as you can see from these stories, the right thing differs based on the situation. The important thing is to consider what will work best for the two of you. Explore the options; don't assume that you don't have any. Even if you can't afford regular help, consider reaching out to support groups and offering to trade care. Bring the two people needing help together for a few hours with one spouse spending time with them while the other catches a break. Getting support and help from others in a similar situation can be a lifesaver. In many cases, you'll find support groups/networks nearby. Seek them out.

Consider paying for a break with in-home respite care or even short-term nursing homes when the care needed is beyond your ability or when you need to get away. In many communities, you can find adult care centers and programs. Many have day programs that give you time to yourself on a regular basis. Seek them out.

While caring for someone else, be mindful of your own health. Nurses will tell you how hard the job is, but when it's a loved one, you don't get to go home at the end of your shift. You need sleep, you need to eat well. Take breaks frequently. Manage demands. This can be difficult if the health issue is dementia or other mental issues, but often, in these cases, sleep or TV can stand in for you while you take a break. Watch your own mental health. Many people experience depression and despair during times like these. Depression won't just make you feel bad; it also depresses your immune system so you will be more susceptible to illness. Be willing to consider short-term counselling or medication.

When friends offer help, take it. Be ready to propose specific tasks that would most help you. Many find just getting away for an hour or two helps the most. Don't be afraid to ask. What do you need most that you can't easily do for yourself? Check on new support options and technologies. You may find help there. Just as smart speakers, such as those made by Apple and Amazon, solve the problem of children constantly asking "why," similar technology may help give you space.

To make life simpler, even before anything happens make sure you have a good system for organizing your health information and legal documents. If you don't have a trust/will, get that done now. If your documents are dated, get them updated. Laws change, and you want to make sure you have everything in order, including a durable power of attorney for healthcare and another for financial matters.

In some cases, the caregiving stint could be relatively short-term, such as with some strokes or cancers. When you know there's an end in sight, it might make the job easier. You can see progress and celebrate each small victory. For caregivers dealing with chronic or terminal diseases, the demands and stresses will be greater. You'll need to make sure you get the support you need.

Most of us find it difficult to ask for help, while being happy to help others. I share that challenge, but try to keep reminding myself: when you can help someone, it feels great to be able to make a difference. When we fail to ask for help, we're depriving others of the chance to be of service and have that good feeling. Ask. When you're clear and specific on what you need, you'll be pleasantly surprised at how much support you have. Think of what your friends and family do best. When you need a meal, ask your favorite home chef. Get a passionate reader to come over to read out loud. If your spouse loves to binge watch TV, find your friends who share the passions and invite them over for a few hours. Having people to rely on in trying times is yet another reason to maintain your contacts and build relationships.

Recognize that caregiving is the hardest job you'll ever have, and be cognizant of your successes and forgiving of your failures. Everyone gets angry at loved ones when the demands become too great. Expect that you'll do your best and forget about perfection.

Chapter 19

Divorce

When people divorce, it's always such a tragedy.
At the same time, if people stay together
it can be even worse.
—Monica Bellucci, actress and model

Depending on the kind of work you're doing or have done in the past, some people have found that their marriage worked, in part, because they spent so little time together. Raising children, long commutes, and frequent travel can limit the time a couple spends together. In retirement, depending on your plans, you'll probably be spending more time together. It may surprise you to discover that some relationship assumptions don't stand up to being in constant, close proximity to each other.

My husband spent his career as an airline pilot, which meant being gone much of the time. In fact, he had several year-long contract jobs where he couldn't get home until the contract finished. We often laughed at the idea that his many absences made the heart grow fonder, and we loved our reconnections. Still, it meant we didn't spend a lot of time together. I wondered what would happen when he retired, especially as I would still be working from home. We quickly discovered that we thrived through the transition. When he's busy typing, it spurs me to work more consistently and harder. We share things throughout the day. Surprising both of us, we now spend very little time apart. But it doesn't work that way for everyone.

Sang commuted from Brentwood to Silicon Valley, a trip that frequently took two hours in the morning and more at night. His wife, Chau, worked as a nurse in town, and their kids had done well in local schools. Both had dreamed of living closer to San Francisco, but couldn't afford the kind of house they wanted in that area. When the children moved out and they began retirement plans, they agreed to downsize.

Sang felt he should have more say in the decision. After all, he had given up so much to let Chau have a short commute and be able to spend more time with their kids. Chau admitted she had felt like a single parent, with all the responsibilities and no time for herself.

They began to fight over everything. Sang wanted a small apartment in San Francisco, where they could enjoy the arts and nightlife. Chau dreamed of a small farm, perhaps in another state. Sang looked forward to sleeping in and doing nothing when he felt like it. He wanted to feel free of obligations. Chau wanted to have their grandkids around, even considering moving to be near one family so they could provide day care. She also loved to get up early and start the day with her chores, waking Sang with her activities.

With some hesitation, they sought marriage counseling. They felt that such a long marriage couldn't possibly end just because they no longer had work distractions. Over time, it became clear that they really had very little in common. The needs of their children had been the bridge that connected them. With the children gone and Sang home all the time, their differences became apparent. They decided to divorce.

Financial discussions increased the acrimony. Under California law, Sang found he had to give up 50% of his 401-K to Chau because she had never saved any of her income. He knew they had to split the house, but felt that with his greater contribution to paying the mortgage, he should have a bigger share. In addition, due to their long years of marriage, he found himself on the hook for alimony. His anger grew.

Chau felt like a beggar, arguing for every cent. She worried that she would have to go back to nursing, even as she felt she didn't have the stamina to continue as she had been. They both realized that they didn't really want to spend their remaining years alone, but hadn't maintained a lot of friendships other than with other couples. Dating late in life seemed like an insurmountable challenge. And yet, they knew they couldn't make their marriage work.

After the divorce, they found they could maintain a friendly but distant acquaintanceship, which made keeping up with their kids much easier.

"We're better apart than together," Chau said, surprised at the realization. "We've lost the love and found the 'like'."

Divorce late in life can be devastating. When you've shared your life with someone, you've built all your memories together. You've blended everything and learned to accommodate each other's differences. But now that you've aged, your energy and perception of your personal attractiveness may be on the wane. Some may find they're perfectly happy living on their own. If marital strife had been a stressor, a divorce may be even more freeing than retirement. But it is always costly. Two people living together simply spend less than two living on their own, unless the divorce resulted from one partner being a spendthrift.

While we can't prepare for this eventuality, we can consider what will happen when we have to live alone. It's rare for a couple to die at the same time, and while divorce is more complex, in most cases it is death that will separate us from our spouse. While making plans for your life alone, you're also planning for what you'd do in a divorce. Life on your own has challenges, but it also may mean opportunities. Compromises are a part of any marriage; when you're alone, you make all the decisions. You may have had unrealized goals that you've ignored. It's time to take action on them.

Grieving takes time. You have to give yourself the space to recover, whether the loss is due to divorce or death. Mourning is personal. No one can tell you how long it should go on or how quickly you can get your feet back under you. Crisis centers, counseling, and support groups can make a difference. You don't have to do this alone. As you move through the phases of grief, you'll restart your life better if you've saved up some deferred dreams.

This means that, when you are crafting plans for an ideal retirement, there may be ideas that you and your spouse don't share. If you can't do them on your own while still married, save them up. You might find the possibilities help you move forward and return to your usual state of positivity. Many studies have proven that we older folks are happier than any other age group. Part of this is resilience, which was learned the hard way over our roller coaster lives. But another part is our ability to enjoy ourselves and understand what pleasure means to us. It's still there, even after a loss. Concrete plans help reacquaint you with your smile.

If you still want to be part of a couple, the options are better than ever. Sites like Our Time match older singles. With age comes a better understanding of who we are and what we want in a relationship. Being alone may be a refreshing change, but if it isn't, you can find another person to share part or all of your life. Others find that friendship is all they seek. More and more, you'll see two men or two women traveling together, enjoying both the cost savings and the companionship. The options for friendship, relationship and love are as varied as your imagination.

Chapter 20

Adapting to Your Own Aging

Aging is an extraordinary process where you become the person you always should have been.
—David Bowie, musician

I had a completely erroneous idea about physical and mental aging. I imagined a slow ride down the slope from my peak with no perceptible change until one day, you wake up and think "Wow, I can barely touch my toes anymore." Or, "The only things I can remember are the lyrics of songs I never liked." As I got older, I also pushed out the age at which I would consider myself "old." Don't we all do this? Saying that 60 is the new 40 only sounds funny for so long. Can we really think that 70 is the new 40?

At some point, you have to embrace your age. For me, 65 represented my favorite birthday (so far) because the year had so much going for it. We planned more travel for that year than ever before. In every way, the work I still did was work I loved. I got to get on Medicare, a huge win for the self-employed. At the same time, I began to realize that life's "takeaways" came more in dramatic changes than in barely noticed small insults. I remember at 60 when I fell and hurt my knee. It seemed like a meniscus tear, an injury I hadn't previously experienced, but had seen other people incur when they fell as I did. Instead, to my shock, my sports medicine doctor told me that I had bone-on-bone arthritis of the knee. In fact, even though only one knee hurt, both knees had pretty severe damage.

In one visit, I went from being a healthy athlete to a person who needed to protect my knees. No more high impact Jazzer-cise, an activity I loved. It took months to convert to and enjoy low-impact. I liken aging now to periods of a holding pattern punctuated by bigger losses. Nouns and names elude me, only to reappear hours later when they only annoy me. Am I the only person wishing we all had to wear name-tags?

I'm lucky. Most of my age-related maladies are treatable or bearable. Not everyone has this good fortune. And those of us not yet experiencing something awful may find that the big changes lie just around the corner.

Marla had designed the perfect life for herself. She taught exercise classes and gave massages in Portland. Great at her job, she had been able to put her daughter, Jennifer, through college, and now looked forward to her daughter's wedding. She loved the man her daughter had chosen, a fact that con-cerned her as she feared that her positive regard for the man might put Jennifer off. A few weeks before the wedding, she went for her annual mammogram and learned that she had a worrying lump. Terrified, she put off the needle biopsy, telling herself that she just wanted to enjoy the wedding and not worry anyone.

Scolded by her doctor for the delay, she finally went in for what she assumed would be a quick procedure followed by good news. Waking up hours later, she found herself minus a breast. Chemotherapy followed. She struggled to get her life back on track, discovering quickly that she couldn't continue the jobs she loved. Her muscle strength never fully rebounded; a single massage would knock her back. Healthy for so many years, she'd never thought about alternatives. But she loved to work, and only really felt herself when she had a chance to help others.

As she worked through physical therapy, she talked to her therapist about her work. Ken suggested she consider creating classes just for mastectomy survivors. As long as she pitched it as exercise rather than using the term "physical therapy," he felt certain she could make it work without additional training.

"I'll send people your way," he said. "Most of my patients really need to keep at it much longer than insurance will cover. It's hard to motivate yourself to do the work at home. A class would really make a difference for them."

Marla created the class and found herself surprised at how even former exercise students showed up to work with her. Many wanted personal training, and she decided to get the certification so she could do a great job for them. As she demonstrated moves and pushed herself as well as her students, her stamina increased, as did her muscle tone. One day, looking at herself in the mirror, something she had managed to avoid for months, she discovered that she looked the way she had looked before the surgery, minus the breast. While she had initially planned to get her breast replaced, she decided the scar marked something important for her: a mark of strength and heroism.

One day, she found a man standing around her studio. It took him several minutes, but he confessed that he had had breast cancer too. He couldn't face even the small amount of public notice at his physical therapist's gym, and his PT had recommended her. "I'd prefer a private class," Daniel said.

After a few weeks, his confidence grew and he joined her all-girls class. They immediately adopted him, enjoying having a nice-looking man around. After a few months, when he had regained strength and confidence, Daniel asked Marla out. She hesitated, but got on board when he slayed her with a jokey comment.

"C'mon. Two breasts are better than one."

In that moment, she realized that not only had she helped him heal. She could laugh again too.

Health issues can be major or minor, but when they happen to you, you may find yourself needing someone to care for you. Most of my friends never had children, so that option is closed to them, but even those who reproduced may find they can't look in that direction for support. If your spouse is gone when you need help, this is one area you have to plan for. Talk to your financial advisor early on in retirement to plan for this kind of expense. Options beyond long-term care insurance are available. Know what you want in the event you need care, so you can define your living situation. This is where the CCRC living situation really can make a difference for a lot of people, but remember that you can't get into one of these after you are diagnosed with any of a large number of excluding illnesses and conditions.

Minor health issues can impact you as well. We all know that, at some point, we won't be able to drive. This usually starts with not feeling safe driving at night. I know that between wearing contacts and having a car that sits lower to the ground, the glare of SUV and truck lights means I limit my night driving to short trips. While my family regularly left for a vacation at 2 AM, I no longer plan this kind of a trip. I do feel safe driving to the airport in the middle of the night, but only because traffic is light at that time. Does the community you live in provide good transportation options? Do you have delivery services like Instacart and DoorDash to help you out with food? Knowing in advance the kinds of support your community provides to seniors can really help out; you have the information in advance of your need.

I've found it useful to have relationships with doctors and pharmacies, even though I don't use either all that much. Your pharmacist should know about all your medications as they can use an intelligent program to look at possible drug interactions. They are the first place to call if you think you're having a medication issue, but they're also great resources when you get a minor illness or injury and want help in deciding what to buy. Make use of them. Most really enjoy the chance to be more than just a "prescription-filler", and they have much more training on medications than your doctor.

Over the course of a few sports injuries, I've had the opportunity to use physical therapy. Now, you can save money and time by creating your own physical therapy support center. You can purchase all kinds of useful things such as therapy tape (videos online show you how to use it), ultrasound machine, and TENS units, all of which can help minor injuries heal faster. Once you've gone through some exercises for a condition and understand how to get the most from them, you can just do them at home. It can feel empowering to know that you can handle a variety of medical situations on your own.

For travelers, start creating a medical kit to take on trips. Having a few things with you can save a vacation; in some places, it can be hard to find things that you need to quickly recover from an illness or food poisoning, even if you can find someone who speaks your language. However, if you can find a helpful soul who understands your needs, you may find a new remedy. Laws and approvals differ in various countries, and I've had a few really great remedies offered to me in countries like Germany and France, some of which I can't get in the US.

Create a list of support people to call in an emergency. You might not really need 911 and an ambulance. Older people can support each other; create a call circle so that you have the names and numbers stored both on paper and on your phone before you need them. Since so many people rely on cell phones now, also make sure you have a backup charging unit in case the emergency includes a power outage.

So much else could be covered in this chapter, but it's the right place to mention that you need to be sure to have a trust, pour-over will, final instructions, health care directive, and a durable power of attorney for healthcare and finance all in place. If you have them, check them regularly as life changes occur. It brings peace of mind to know that you've ensured that your wishes will be followed. Many of my friends deprived themselves of a good retirement trying to build an estate for their children. If you have some extra, give it to them now so you can see them enjoy it. Go through your jewelry and give your long unworn pieces to your family. Enjoy watching them wear your good jewels. For me and for many of you, remember: if your children love you, they want you to have what you need in retirement. The only thing they might want after you die is a picture or treasured memento. If they care about your estate, they probably don't deserve to get it.

None of us knows what tomorrow will bring. All we can do is be prepared and ready to meet the challenge as we've successfully met all those throughout our lives. Be prepared for the worst while enjoying the longer, happier lifespan most of us will achieve. It's going to be a great ride!

Conclusion

The well-planned life is a life you will enjoy. As we always said in diving, "Failure to plan is planning to fail." I hope that this book offered you some insights into the kinds of things you might want to consider as you plan to retire. Even if you've already pulled the plug on your lifetime of work, it may serve you to reconsider all your options. We're only going to get a few great years before health issues begin to reduce our options; let's make them really great.

Start by dreaming big, imagining all the things you've always thought about doing.

So many of our dreams at first seem impossible,
then they seem improbable, and then,
when we summon the will, they soon become inevitable.
—Christopher Reeve, actor

Acknowledgements

Some people say that writing is a lonely task, but for an extrovert like me, I have to make it social. I've enjoyed interviewing and chatting with people about their retirement plans; the issues they raised inspired this book. Working with my retirement coaching clients also gave me powerful insights into what was missing from the books already out there.

Critique groups are essential; we can't really judge our own work, nor can we anticipate how it comes across to others. Shout-outs to some great writers and members of various groups along the way: Suzanne Arbil, Lloyd Lofthouse, Kalyani Deshpande, Heidi Eliason, Alicia Watson and Nancy Hume. Your honest feedback shaped my view of this work and helped me hone it.

My beta readers made a big difference; they were the first to see the book as a whole. Thanks to MaryAnne Cacciola, Linda Donovan, Eric Tesinsky and Heidi Eliaison for reading my book so carefully and giving me such great feedback. The book is better for your help.

My husband, Mike, has been a part of this from the beginning. He retired much earlier than me, showing me how a life phase we anticipate with such pleasure can also present challenges. His encouragement kept me going.

I should have this in all my books, but I have to thank my high school English teacher, Ruth Protter. More than anyone, she held me to high standards while shoring up my confidence.

Thanks also to the people who make this into a book that readers can actually access: my copy editor, Don Maker and my publisher, Alive Book Publishing. Without them, I wouldn't be free to just be creative and write.

Thank you, readers. Let this inspire you to take the next steps to making your retirement great. You can reach out to me at denise@dpkcoaching, Tweet with me at @denisekalm and find my other books on http://www.denisekalm.com. I'd love to hear from you.

APPENDICES

Appendix A
Medicare Basics

Medicare offers great medical coverage, but your first open enrollment is going to be more challenging than any you faced while employed. You'll have a lot to choose from. The good news is that you have time to prepare. But wait too long and you may find yourself locked in for as much as a year to a plan that doesn't match your needs. Get it right and you'll enjoy lower-cost, quality health care.

You'll be advised that you can enroll for the first time three months before your start date, which is the first day of the month during which you turn 65, not your actual birthday. It's best to get started much sooner. If you do this, you'll be ready to enroll in your plan(s) at the three-month mark, ensuring you get all the paperwork and cards back on time.

Research begins with the many free seminars offered, especially during open enrollment in November and December. Though you can find seminars offered at other times, more options are available then. You'll learn about them through mailers and newspaper ads, but you can also search them out. Medicare.gov has tools to help you isolate which plans are available in your area. This site also helps you compare pricing very easily. Still, the plans require study, and the seminars give you a chance to ask questions.

Attend a few seminars to learn the basics; you get a different perspective from different insurance agents. In some areas, Medicare classes may be offered; take the time to learn as much as possible so that you understand all your choices. These classes and the Medicare site are particularly helpful if you plan to work past age 65. In that case, your choices will be different than if you intend to rely on Medicare for all your health needs (see section below.) In any event, collect the brochures and plan descriptions offered. You'll want time to compare them at your leisure.

When it comes time to pick an agent to work with, make sure they are independent. If you pick one that is tied to an insurance company, that's all they can sell. Although it might be the one you want, if your circumstances change, you may need to change agents. It's easier if you have an agent who can present you with a variety of choices.

Another big decision is whether you want Medicare Advantage or MediGap (Medicare Supplement.) The former is an HMO plan, which offers benefits, but only with a restricted group of doctors and hospitals. For many already on an HMO, this can be an easy choice, but check the prices. What might have been less expensive for you as an employee may be the higher cost option now. Medicare Advantage takes care of all of your plan choices, once you pick a company. You'll still have to sign up for Medicare as noted in the next paragraph, but you'll have all your benefits through your Advantage company. Most plans include your drug coverage, but many also cover other nice benefits like hearing, vision and more.

During open enrollment (and three months after), you can change from one Advantage plan to another. You can also opt to go back into basic Medicare and add Medigap and Plan D, but there may be underwriting involved.

Medigap plans work well for those who are less comfortable with the HMO style plan, which usually requires co-pays for a lot of your health needs and will restrict the doctors and hospitals you can use. Most people will have several options for these plans. Medigap will cover any doctor who takes Medicare, and may cover part of the payment for those who don't. You will need Part D (drug coverage) as it isn't included. Note: even if you don't take medication or your medication is inexpensive, you need to sign up for a plan. For every month you don't take it, you'll pay a penalty for delaying, just as you will if you delay Part B. Almost all of us will end up needing more expensive drugs as we age, so sign up for the least expensive plan right away.

Next, you have to pick the type of plan you want. No matter which insurance company you select, each of the plan types will cover the same thing as listed in the chart below. Starting in 2020, Plan F will no longer be available. Most people opt for Plan G or N, unless they can't afford the higher priced plans. If you check out the chart, you'll see that you pay less for everything with the higher priced plans. For traveling seniors, F and G offer foreign travel emergency help. Your first year, you can pick any plan and will not have to provide any medical information.

Keep in mind that, unlike Advantage, supplemental plans are not as easy to change. If you want to change during open enrollment, you may need to fill out a medical questionnaire (underwriting), and you may be rejected if you have a lot of medical issues. Picking the right plan can make a big difference. In some states, you can change on your birthday without underwriting. If the premium goes up beyond a certain percentage or if you move, you may have more flexibility. The challenges around changing policies mean it's important to have an agent working with you; they can help you assess your options, if you wish to change.

Medigap Benefits Chart	Plan A	Plan B	Plan C	Plan D	Plan F	Plan G	Plan K	Plan L	Plan M	Plan N
Medicare Part A Coinsurance & Hospital Costs (Up to an additional 365 days after Medicare benefits are used) are used up	100%	100%	100%	100%	100%	100%	100%	100%	100%	100%
Medicare Part B Coinsurance or Copayment	100%	100%	100%	100%	100%	100%	50%	75%	100%	100%
Blood (First 3 Pints)	100%	100%	100%	100%	100%	100%	50%	75%	100%	100%
Part A Hospice Care Coinsurance or Copayment	100%	100%	100%	100%	100%	100%	50%	75%	100%	100%
Skilled Nursing Facility Coinsurance	✗	✗	100%	100%	100%	100%	50%	75%	100%	100%
Medicare Part A Deductible	✗	100%	100%	100%	100%	100%	50%	75%	50%	100%
Medicare Part B Deductible	✗	✗	100%	✗	100%	✗	✗	✗	✗	✗
Medicare Part B Excess Charges	✗	✗	✗	✗	100%	100%	✗	✗	✗	✗
Foreign Travel Emergency (up to plan limits)	✗	✗	80%	80%	80%	80%	✗	✗	80%	80%
					** Out of Pocket Limit		$5,560	$2,780		

Fig 3. Benefit Choices

Everyone will want Part A – the hospital plan. It's free. You should take Part B, though you'll have to pay for it. If you are already enrolled in Social Security, the government will sign you up automatically; they do this because they can get the payment deducted from your monthly Social Security amount. If you aren't on Social Security, you'll need to do this yourself. While it might seem obvious to register at medicare.gov, that's not where you sign up. Instead, you want https://www.ssa.gov/benefits/retirement/. If you go to the basic Social Security page and login, you look for retirement options, then scroll down to find where you can enroll in Medicare. On the home page, it isn't obvious. If you haven't set up an account (and you should have because you no longer get printed annual statements and have to get them online), you'll need to set up an account before you can enroll.

Fill out all the information and prepare to wait. It can take as long as a month to get your card. While you'll get the benefits on that first day of the month no matter what, it's a lot easier with the card and a number. Most of the time, you'll need your Medicare number to apply for Medigap and Part D, so applying for A and B is your first step.

As you've seen, an agent can be an important choice. They will be there to help you assess your options, and often have tools and videos to help you make the right choice. While your instinct might be to check Yelp and pick a local agent, you don't need to do that. Most interactions are by email and phone, so look until you find someone you can work with who represents all the plans you might consider. Along the way, I discovered Boomer Benefits, http://www.boomerbenefits.com, a Texas-based insurance agency founded in 2005 to simply the process of applying and benefiting from Medicare. Although I had enjoyed talking with some local agents, this agency offered far more assistance. I worked with one agent by phone and she provided me with quick answers, lots of information on the site, and quick videos that answered all my questions. Together, we quickly filled out my Medigap form on the phone. Boomer Benefits also offers to help you if you have issues with Medicare itself, as in cases where you aren't getting the benefits you think you should be getting. Not all agents are there for you after enrollment. You'll also want someone to check in with every year to ensure your coverage is what you need.

Livorna had enjoyed a great relationship with her insurance broker for many years, relying on him to find her a variety of insurance products. As she reached 65, she decided to get his help with Medicare. Her small town of Wilmington didn't have a lot of broker options. Since she had always felt she got the best options from this agent, she didn't balk at paying

$90/month for Part D, even as she took only one inexpensive, generic prescription medication. He emphasized how important it would be to enroll in Part D immediately. He only showed the one plan. Months later, she spoke with Maria.

"You're paying what?" Maria asked, stifling a laugh.

"What are you paying?"

"$12.90/month. It's the lowest price plan."

Livorna hadn't checked it out herself, so easy to do on Medicare.gov. And now she felt stuck with a bad plan. Open enrollment was months away.

Nick found himself navigating the Medicare jungle in his 50s as he began to care full-time for his aging mother. Her health had deteriorated, but she had only opted for Part A, unwilling to spend the extra money for anything else. Now, she needed more care and her small pension and Social Security benefits didn't cover much. Nick was horrified to discover that Part B and D would now be much more costly than if she had enrolled earlier. Fortunately, she qualified for some help here, but the mistake was costly. Nick vowed not to repeat the mistake when it became time to enroll himself.

Some of us plan to work past 65. If you work for an employer who has more than 20 employees and you have employer-provided health insurance, you only need to apply for Part A, which won't cost you anything. In this case, Medicare pays second after your regular insurance. After you retire, you'll get a letter from the insurance company letting Medicare know that you don't pay a penalty for late Part B enrollment. As a note, if you have an HSA plan and have been contributing, you can't enroll in Medicare. Check with an agent, but it may be the best plan is to stop the HSA contributions.

If your company is smaller, enroll in Part A and B during the seven-month period around your birthday. If you have been laid off and are using COBRA, enroll in Part A and B.

Medicare will be your primary insurance and COBRA the secondary.

A savvy tip is to make color copies of both sides of your Medicare card and laminate cards you can put in your wallet. The paper original can be stored in your files.

Take the time to learn about your options and make good choices upfront. You'll never regret it. We'll be relying more on our health insurance to help us navigate the heavy waters of aging. Be prepared, protected and safe from unexpected and unwelcome high medical bills.

Appendix B

Phone and Internet Safety

Keeping your identity and your finances safe must be at the top of your mind. Scammers prey on older people, believing us to be more gullible. Sadly, this assumption too often turns out to be true. Though most Baby Boomers are pretty internet savvy, not all of us know the variety of ways that they can be trapped. And the inventive minds of the scammers never cease to come up with new ideas.

Start by being skeptical of anyone asking for money or personal information. One of the latest scams involves a threatening phone call from "the IRS" demanding payment. If you stick on long enough, you find that, improbably, they want payment in iTunes gift cards. A quick check will show you that not only does the IRS never call in a payment situation, they also publicize this scam and warn you against it.

A new twist is the ability for scammers to spoof phone numbers. You'll see a call from your local area and be more open to it. Jot the number down and try to call it; spoofed numbers don't ring through. If the caller offers something attractive, tell them that you are in the middle of something and will be happy to call them back. People offering genuine products and services will provide a valid phone number. Scammers never will.

You can register all of your phone numbers with the Do Not Call Registry, but we've found that doesn't seem to help much. Call blocking is helpful with robocalls, although too many still seem to get through. The best involves requiring the caller to key in a number, one that changes for every caller. MagicJack service provides this, as do a few phone companies. Nomorobo provides a service that works with most existing phone systems. After you sign up, you will get a single ring, followed by the system hanging up on them. If it doesn't work, check with your phone provider. Some of them need to flip a switch to enable this feature. You'll still get more sophisticated scammers, but it definitely cuts down on the numbers. I still smile when I hear the hang-ups.

Sometimes, a caller will offer a service you're actually thinking might be useful. Get their website and call-back number. Do some homework. Yelp and HomeAdvisor can offer reviews. The Better Business Bureau may give you more information. Don't deal with anyone you can't vet, no matter how good the price.

The internet is a trickier platform. It's impossible to surf without being willing to be tracked through "cookies," which give good guys and scammers information about your interests. The only defense is how you deal with them when they contact you. However, if you want to be safer, make sure you have an anti-virus solution installed and regularly updated. To increase your security, particularly to avoid getting tracked or having someone hijack your computer, invest in a router (some ISPs offer them with the service, but they aren't expensive) and choose a virtual private network (VPN). Make sure to put a password on your router so that people can't hijack their way into your system. Both routers and VPNs offer a lot of protection. In addition, hardwire the devices you do financial work through, such as online banking. When you are using WiFi, you're far more exposed. Someone walking near you or even just outside your house may be able to hack in through your WiFi. You might also want to look into anonymous search engines, like DuckDuckGo, especially if you want to keep your browsing secret.

Hackers still use old-school scams, such as the Nigerian

scam where they offer you a huge settlement, provided you send them a few hundred dollars. Most end up in your spam folder, but some make it through. However, more insidious techniques can cause you problems. Clicking on links, even those sent to you by friends, is hazardous. Make sure you look at the link AND the sending email. Even though it may say your friend sent it, does the email address match? If you get sent a YouTube video link and they tell you what it's about, consider going to YouTube and searching on the topic.

Many times, you'll get an email sent to a lot of people purportedly from a friend. In most cases, only the link appears. This generally means the sender had his address list hijacked and, if you click on the link, yours will be too. You may not even realize the exposure. What I do is create a new email for that friend and let them know that this has happened, so they can run a virus scan. Another friend scam is the email that indicates that your friend has been traveling and was robbed. The request is for money to help bail them out of this bad situation. Often, it's someone you haven't heard from in years; that's the easy case, because you know they wouldn't be asking you. But even when it's a friend, check with them directly first, if you can. For most people, trying to get a friend to send you money shouldn't be the first option anyway. Never send money unless you can verify the situation.

Offers that seem to be too good to be true or come unsolicited should be viewed as suspicious. I've had career coaching clients get surprisingly good job offer emails; when you're searching hard for a well-paying job, it's easy to get sucked in. Always do your homework. Vacation awards often work the same way. If you didn't enter a contest but get an email offering you a vacation, be skeptical. How do they even know you? If the offer looks attractive, check it out in the background. Does the company exist? Is the email from a company address or from Gmail? And never give banking information in an email or online, unless you have a verified site that begins: https. Even some charities still don't have secure sites; if you want to donate, just call them.

One way to protect your email address list from hacking is to have a non-working address as the first one. This should break down the auto-sender. You might list A Big Idiot with the email address abi@noservice.com. There may be ways around this, but it works in many cases.

Be vigilant with your PC or Mac. If something looks strange, run a deep scan. Check to see if a new Windows or iOS has been installed; this may cause some appearance changes. Take it to an expert. You know what you should see, so if things have changed, be skeptical. And make sure to invest in Cloud backup. Even if the worst happens, you can go to the Cloud and invoke what I call "the WayBack Machine," which will reset you back to where you were before someone got in.

Be aware of your credit rating. Where it used to be a major effort to get the number, now, most credit cards offer it on a regular basis, and you're entitled to a credit report yearly from each of the three agencies. Some hacks aren't detectable until you see what's happening on your credit. Keep on top of it.

Change passwords and make use of the special characters and numbers to make them harder to guess. The more you do, the harder you are to hack. When I lived in Oakland, I worried about break-ins. The policeman I talked to said that your goal isn't to be impregnable; no one can be. You simply need to be more annoying than other people to discourage criminals. Unless you have some rare art object or valuable jewelry, you aren't a target. Make it tough for them to get to you and, most likely, they'll turn to the next person.

Appendix C

My Supplements

I thought it might be useful to get an idea of what I take to maintain my health and why. I'm not suggesting you follow it, but it might inspire some new choices if you hadn't realized how much you can do to help yourself. It sounds like a lot (and it is), but I'm a bit of a health nut. If I'm going to live longer, I want them to be healthy years, not time in a care unit. However, what I do isn't for everyone.

Before beginning any vitamins, supplements or alternative medicines, check with your doctor. Many can interact with drugs you're already taking or cause problems with pre-existing health issues. Just because you don't need a prescription for something doesn't mean it's totally safe. When selecting supplements, do some homework to make sure you're getting exactly what you're paying for. There's not a lot of regulation in the industry, and some brands may not serve you as well.

Senior or 50+ multi-vitamin - these are designed to supplement what older people need.

Super B complex - Most of us don't get enough fruit and vegetables. B vitamins help me feel a lot more energetic.

CA citrate, Magnesium and Zinc - essential for bone health. Increasingly, people are discovering the need for more calcium and magnesium.

D3 - Will help your muscles, bones, digestion, immunity, hormones and circulation keep functioning well. It may also help to prevent breast and colon cancer.

Flaxseed - High in omega-3 fatty acids, it has been shown to have several health benefits, such as reduced blood pressure and improved regularity.

Fish Oil - Makes your cell membranes healthier. Use of fish oil has been known to ward off depression, ease arthritis, protect against dementia, and more.

CoQ10 - For heart health and possibly also to increase energy levels. Cholesterol meds can deplete levels, so it's even more important to supplement if you're taking this kind of drug.

Ameal Peptide - Helps stabilize blood pressure.

Lutein, Bilberry and Xeazanthin - For eye health.

Pycnogenol - Good for treating circulation problems, allergies, asthma, ringing in the ears, high blood pressure, muscle soreness, pain, osteoarthritis, diabetes, attention deficit-hyperactivity disorder (ADHD), menopausal symptoms, and more.

Probiotics - Helps to reduce stress and bone loss. Also, a healthy gut means better digestion. With the gut being a second brain, we want to help it thrive as well. Probiotics repopulate your gut.

Estroven - For menopausal symptoms. May also stave off the need to take HRT (hormone replacement therapy).

Multi Supplements for Joint Issues – Glucosamine, Chondroitin Sulfate, MSM, Boswellia, Turmeric – It's possible to find a supplement that contains all of these, but in general you'll have to take it three times a day. But it does seem to help joint lubrication and reduce pain and swelling. If you're trying to put off knee or hip surgery, this may work for you.

Metamucil - For digestive health. I never get enough fiber from my food.

Great sources will be places like Costco or other big box stores, Swanson Vitamins (online), Amazon, etc. Shop around. Stores like CVS and Walgreens often have periodic sales offering buy one, get one free.

Appendix D
Useful Links

http://www.socialsecurity.gov/retire2/agereduction.htm
- calculate what you get based on year of birth

Ch 5 – Values Inventory tools
https://bhmt.org/wpcontent/uploads/2016/04/BHMT_CC_Life-Values_Inventory.pdf - PDF for self-scoring
https://www.valuescentre.com/our-products/products-individuals/personal-values-assessment-pva - online tool

Ch 9 – Volunteering
https://fathomaway.com/24-best-global-volunteer-opportunities/ - combine travel and volunteering
https://www.moneycrashers.com/good-places-volunteer-opportunities-organizations/ - general volunteer opportunities
https://www.aarp.org/giving-back/volunteering/info-12-2011/volunteer-opportunities-with-benefits.html - AARP's ideas
https://www.rd.com/advice/work-career/volunteer-opportunities/ - a few more
http://idealist.org – US and abroad opportunities

Ch 11 – Health
http://www.choosingwisely.org/patient-resources - Useful info on what tests, treatments or procedures are recommended
(or not) for various health conditions.
https://www.health.com/health/article/0,,20411397,00.html

– Input on healthy diets. The key is to find one you can live with. It's not a temporary eating regimen; it's your life.
https://comparativeguide.com/ - Help in picking supplements that will be safe and effective.
https://www.latimes.com/science/sciencenow/la-sci-sn-hidden-drugs-in-supplements-20181016-story.html - Some food for thought about unregulated supplements.

Ch 13 – Creativity tools
http://www.paintnite.com
- Painting classes to explore new ways to create.
https://www.doodlebuddy.co/
- Ways to be creative on devices.
http://www.debonogroup.com/six_thinking_hats.php - In part for corporations, but still an interesting place to look.
https://www.mindtools.com/pages/main/newMN_CT.htm - Some creativity ideas.

Ch – 16
https://www.letter-exchange.com/ - The Letter Exchange – how to find penpals

Ch 18 – Caretaking
https://www.aplaceformom.com/ - living options
https://www.care.com/ - caregiver directory
https://dailycaring.com/ - more resources
http://www.usa.gov - Search on caregiver support. Lots of good information including resources, support, money guidance.
https://amac.us/ - Conservative senior site – alternative to AARP.
https://www.aarp.org/ - Another general senior site.
https://www.alz.org/ - Alzheimer's information
https://archrespite.org/ - Resources for caregivers.

Denise P. Kalm, BCC, has been reinventing herself her entire life, beginning her career in genetics, moving to IT and then training as a personal/executive coach at John F. Kennedy University and as a creativity coach by Eric Maisel. Retirement is her next reinvention; she created this book to help others (and herself) design a retirement of their dreams. She is a published author; a novel, *Lifestorm*, *Career Savvy – Keeping & Transforming Your Job*, *Tech Grief – Survive and Thrive Through Career Losses* (with Linda Donovan) and *First Job Savvy – Find a Job, Start Your Career* are available on all major sites as paperbacks and e-books.

Web sites: www.dpkcoaching.com and www.denisekalm.com.

ABOOKS

ALIVE Book Publishing and ALIVE Publishing Group
are imprints of Advanced Publishing LLC,
3200 A Danville Blvd., Suite 204, Alamo, California 94507

Telephone: 925.837.7303
alivebookpublishing.com

www.ingramcontent.com/pod-product-compliance
Lightning Source LLC
Chambersburg PA
CBHW021333090426
42742CB00008B/592